중학 내신만점

영문법 쏙쏙·영어 쑥쑥

땅편

저자 동영상 강의 예정
www.seeenglish.com

시잉글리쉬
www.seeenglish.com

중학 내신만점
영문법 쏙쏙 · 영어 쑥쑥 (땅편)

초판 발행: 2016년 1.1일

지은이 · 손 창 연
펴낸이 · 손 창 연
표지디자인 · 전 철 규
내지디자인 · 필커뮤니케이션
인쇄 · 송죽문화사
펴낸곳 · **시잉글리쉬**
서울 서초구 양재동 106-6 정오 B/D 402호(우 137-891)
Tel: [02] 573-3581
등록번호 제 22- 2733호
Homepage: **www.seeenglish.com**

ISBN:

정가: 13,000원

들어가는 _ 말

무엇이든 기본이 중요하다.

영어를 가르치기 시작한지도 20여년이 넘었다. 그 동안 중고생들과 대학생 및 성인 등에게 TOEFL, TOEIC, 편입영어, 수능, 중고생 내신 등을 가르치면서 느낀 점은 역시 '기본이 중요하다'라는 것이다. 특히 영어문법은 처음 시작할 때 제대로 배워야 한다는 생각이다.

이 책은 영어를 학습하는 중학생을 위한 책이다. 상위권 초등 5,6학년에게도 어렵지 않다. 학교 영어수업을 이해하고 영어시험에 빈틈없이 준비할 수 있도록 했다. 또한 영어의 기본을 확실하게 하고자 했다.

모든 공부나 세상의 일들이 그렇듯이 영어라는 바다에 나가 자유롭게 항해하기 위해서는 영어단어 하나하나를 꼼꼼히 읽히고, 아주 기초적인 문장에 대한 이치를 정확하게 읽혔을 때, 풍랑에도 안전하게 항해 할 수 있는 진정한 영어실력을 갖출 수 있다.

로마가 하루 아침에 이루어 지지 않았듯이(Rome wasn't built in a day.) 영어도 하루 아침에 이루어 질 수 있는 것이 아니다. 긴 시간동안 끊임없는 암기와 이해, 반복적인 학습이 필요하다.

이 책에서 제시하는 내용을 꼼꼼히 잘 읽히고 문제를 풀어나가다 보면, 자기도 모르는 사이 영어실력이 부쩍 늘었다는 것을 알게 될 것이다.

끝으로 이 책으로 학습하는 모든 학생들이 단 한번 밖에 없는 인생에서 자신의 꿈을 이루고, 인류의 평화와 자유, 그리고 민주주의를 위해 각각의 그릇에 맞는 기여를 하길 기원한다.

2016년 1월 1일
저자 손 창 연

이 책의 _ **공부 방법**

쫄지 말고 열공 ^^

[이 책을 이렇게 공부하자.]

◆ 학습자의 수준에 따라 다르겠지만 작은 챕터는 하루에 하나 긴 챕터는 2~3일에 정복해보자.

◆ 각 챕터의 핵심개념을 정확히 이해 한다. 또 해당 예문을 꼼꼼히 익힌다.

◆ '확인문제'를 통하여 핵심개념을 심화하고 순발력을 강화한다. '확인문제' 문장들도 문제의 답을 찾는데 그치지 않고 각각 해석도 해본다. 언어는 의미파악이 주요 목적이고 문법은 그 의미를 정확하게 하기 위함이다.

◆ 'Reading in Grammar'에서 문제를 풀면서 독해속에서 활용을 해본다.

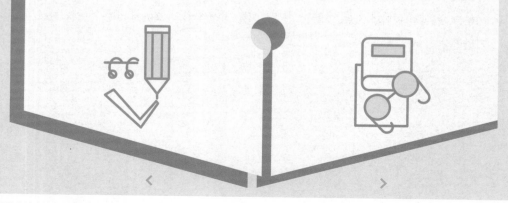

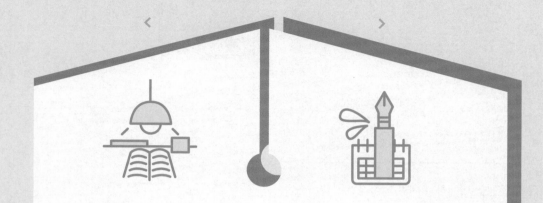

◆ **'중간·기말고사 내신만점대비문제'**를 풀면서 다시 한번 보다 치밀하게 학습한다.

◆ **별책 단어책**의 단원별 단어들을 꼼꼼히 학습하자. 영어학습에서 빼놓을 수 없는 것이 어휘이다. 아무리 설계가 좋고 높은 건물일지라도 벽돌 등 하나하나의 자재 없이 건물은 완성 될 수 없기 때문이다.

◆ 마지막으로 최고의 학습법이자 성공의 팁은 **끈기**다.

기억하자!

[느리지만 꾸준히만 한다면 이길 수 있다.]

Slow but steady wins the race.

이 책의 _ **구성**

Structure

문법핵심 정리와 해설

문법을 이해하기 위한 핵심적인
내용을 예문과 함께 설명했다.

Study 01 부정문

1. 부정문 만드는 법

Pattern 1– be동사/조동사가 있는 경우	Pattern 2– be동사/조동사가 없는 경우
be동사/조동사 not	do/does/did not 동사원형

be동사/조동사 있는 경우

◎ be동사나 조동사 다음에 not만 쓰면 된다.
- Life is a journey.   인생은 여행이다.
  → Life is not a journey.
- Laughter is the best medicine.   웃음은 가장 좋은 약이다.
  → Laughter is not the best medicine.
- Autumn breeze was blowing softly.   가을 산들바람이 부드럽게 불고 있는 중이다.
  → Autumn breeze was not blowing softly.
- President will attend the meeting.   대통령이 회의에 참가 할 것이다.
  → President will not attend the meeting.
- The singer can dance on the big stage.   그 가수는 큰 무대에서 춤 출수 있다.
  → The singer can not dance on the big stage.
- The dancer may go to the banquet.   그 댄서는 연회에 갈 것이다.
  → The dancer may not go to the banquet.
- You should interfere in other's private concerns.   너는 다른 사람의 개인 일에 간섭해야만 한다.
  → You should not interfere in other's private concerns.

확인문제

문법핵심내용을 확인하고 활용하도록
핵심내용을 문제로 풀어보도록 했다.

확인문제 1

다음 각 문제를 부정문으로 고치시오.
(01). Bees are flying insects.
→
(02). Beer is the world's alcoholic beverage.
→
(03). All the medicine is poison.
→
(04). Beer bottle is made of glass.
→
(05). The officials were corrupt.
→
(06). Excess weight can decrease your good cholesterol.
→
(07). You should chew gum in public.
→
(08). Muammar Qaddafi has been killed.
→
(09). The minister will reach the construction site.
→
(10). The ambulance driver will arrive at the hospital soon.
→

Grammar in Reading

배운 내용을 쉬운 지문의 독해속에서도 활용할 수 있도록 어법상 맞지 않는 것을 찾는 문장 등의 문법문제를 출제했다.

Grammar in Reading

4. 다음 ( ) 안에 알맞은 동사를 쓰시오.

Sejin likes to take pictures. A few weeks ago, Sejin ⓐ (show) his pictures to Yuri. She ⓑ (like) them very much. She wanted to take good pictures, too. She asked Sejin for some advice. He ⓒ (give) three tips to her.
First, ⓓ (hold) the camera at the person's eye level, and then move close to the person.
Second, ⓔ (move) the subject from the center of your picture. You can get a better picture that way.
Third, bright sun can make shadows. Turn your flash on, even in the sunshine. You will get a better picture.
Sejin said, "These tips will be helpful. But they are just tips. Take a lot of pictures. You will learn more on your own."
These days, Yuri ⓕ (go) out every weekend with her camera. She really likes to take pictures. It is her new hobby.

01. ⓐ –
02. ⓑ –
03. ⓒ –
04. ⓓ –
05. ⓔ –

중간 · 기말고사 내신만점대비문제

각 단원에서 배운 문법내용을 다시 한번 점검하고 영작 등으로 응용할 수 있도록 했다.
이를 통해 학교 내신시험에 철저히 대비할 수 있는 힘을 기르도록 했다.

중간 · 기말고사 내신만점대비문제

3. 다음 문장의 한글부분을 적절한 의문사를 활용하여 의문문으로 바꾸시오.

01. Bears live 어디에.
→

02. 누구 liked red ripe strawberries.
→

03. Mother Bear made 무엇을.
→

04. 누구가 ate the banana.
→

05. You are 누구를.
→

06. Mom is doing 무엇.
→

07. You like 무슨 animal best.
→

08. His brother likes 무슨 subject best.
→

09. You liked 무슨 과목 best.
→

10. You saw 누구를.
→

11. You married 언제.

중학내신만점 영문법 쏙쏙 · 영어 쑥쑥 〈땅 편〉

Contents

이 책의 _ **차례**

별 책

중학내신만점
영문법 쏙쏙 · 영어 쑥쑥 [하늘편]

하늘편

중학내신만점
영문법 쏙쏙 · 영어 쑥쑥 [바다편]

Chapter

01

Contraction
축약형

Study 01 대명사와 be동사의 결합에 의한 축약

- I am   →   I'm
- He is   →   He's
- She is   →   She's
- It is   →   It's
- That is   →   That's
- We are   →   We're
- You are   →   You're
- They are   →   They're
- There is   →   There's
- How is   →   How's
- What is   →   What's

★ be동사에서 a, i가
각각 '(어포스트로피)가 된다.

다만, **There are**는 There're로 쓰지 않는다. 또 This is는 This's로 쓰지 않는다.

🔍 확인문제 1

다음을 줄여 쓰시오.

(01). I am   → _____

(02). He is   → _____

(03). She is   → _____

(04). It is   → _____

(05). That is   → _____

(06). We are   → _____

(07). You are   → _____

(08). They are   →_____

(09). There is   → _____

(10). How is   → _____

(11). What is   → _____

〈정답과 해설 2P〉

Study 02 대명사와 조동사의 결합에 의한 축약

- We will → We'll
- I would like → I'd like
- I had better → I'd better

★ 조동사에서 wi, woul, ha가
   각각 '(어포스트러피)가 된다.

확인문제 2

다음을 줄여 쓰시오.

(01). We will → _____

(02). I would like → _____

(03). I had better → _____

〈정답과 해설 2P〉

Study 03 대명사와 have동사의 결합에 의한 축약

• I have	→	I've
• We have	→	We've
• You have	→	You've
• They have	→	They've
• He has	→	He's
• She has	→	She's

★ have동사에서 ha가
'(어포스트러피)가 된다.

결국 He's는 He is나 He has의 줄임 형이다.

🔍 확인문제 3

다음을 줄여 쓰시오.

(01). I have → _____

(02). We have → _____

(03). You have → _____

(04). They have → _____

(05). He has → _____

(06). She has → _____

〈정답과 해설 2P〉

Study 04 not이 있는 부정문에서 축약

1. be동사의 양다리 결합

⊙ be동사의 현재형 is나 are는 앞에 온 대명사와 결합하기도 하고 뒤에 온 not과 결합하기도 한다.

He is not → He's not

또는

He is not → He isn't

be동사는 앞의 대명사와 붙을 수도 있고 뒤의 not과 붙을 수도 있다. 만드는 법은 He is에서 He is가 붙으면서 i가 어포스트로피(')가 되어 He's가 된다. 또 is not은 not에서 o가 어포스트로피(')가 되어 isn't가 된다.

마찬가지로 They are에서 a가 어포스토로피(')가 되어 They're가 된다. 또 are not은 not에서 o가 어포스트로피(')가 되어 aren't가 된다.

- **They are** not → They're not
- They **are not** → They aren't

마찬가지로

- She is not   →   She's not   OR   She isn't
- It is not   →   It's not   OR   It isn't
- We are not   →   We're not   OR   We aren't
- You are not   →   You're not   OR   You aren't

다만 am은 대명사(I)하고만 결합한다.

- I am not→ I'm not

확인문제 4

다음을 줄여 쓰시오. 가능한 경우 2가지로 줄여 쓰시오.

(01). I am not → _____

(02). She is not → _____

(03). It is not → _____

(04). We are not → _____

(05). You are not → _____

(06).They are not → _____

〈정답과 해설 2P〉

2. was, were와 not이 결합 축약

I <u>was not</u> → I wasn't

They <u>were not</u> → They weren't

또한 He was not, We were not 등에서는 He, We 등 대명사와 과거형 be동사 was, were는 결합하지 않는다. 대신 be동사는 뒤에 온 not과 결합한다. 이 때 not의 o가 어포스트로피(')가 된다.

• He was not → He wasn't
• She was not → She wasn't
• It was not → It wasn't
• We were not → We weren't
• You were not → We weren't
• They were not → We weren't

★ not에서 o가
'(어포스트러피)가 된다.

확인문제 5

다음을 줄여 쓰시오.

(01). He was not → _____

(02). She was not → _____

(03). It was not → _____

(04). We were not → _____

(05). You were not → _____

(06). They were not → _____

〈정답과 해설 2P〉

3. 조동사와 not의 결합

He <u>does no</u>t → He doesn't

do, does, did나 can, must 등 조동사나 have동사가 나오면 역시 not에서 o가 어포스트로피(')가 되고 축약된다.

- They do not → They don't
- You did not → You didn't
- I have not → I haven't
- He has not → He hasn't
- He can not → He can't
- He must not → He mustn't
- He had not → He hadn't

★ not에서 o가
'(어포스트러피)가 된다.

다만 will not은 won't가 된다.

• We **will not** →We won't

그래서 아래처럼 줄여서 쓰인다.

• I/You/We/They **do** not study → I/You/We/They don't study
• He/She/It **does** not study → He/She/It doesn't study
• I/You/We/They/He/She/It **did** not play → I/You/We/They/He/She/It didn't play
• I/We/They **have** not seen → I/We/They haven't
• He/She/It **has** not read → He/She/It hasn't read

확인문제 6

(01). It did not play　　　→ ＿＿＿＿＿＿＿＿＿＿

(02). We do not　　　　　→ ＿＿＿＿＿＿＿＿＿＿

(03). He does not　　　　→ ＿＿＿＿＿＿＿＿＿＿

(04). We will not　　　　→ ＿＿＿＿＿＿＿＿＿＿　OR ＿＿＿＿＿＿＿＿＿＿

(05). They have not　　　→ ＿＿＿＿＿＿＿＿＿＿　OR ＿＿＿＿＿＿＿＿＿＿

(06). He has not　　　　→ ＿＿＿＿＿＿＿＿＿＿　OR ＿＿＿＿＿＿＿＿＿＿

(07). He can not　　　　→ ＿＿＿＿＿＿＿＿＿＿

(08). He must not　　　→ ＿＿＿＿＿＿＿＿＿＿

(09). He had not　　　　→ ＿＿＿＿＿＿＿＿＿＿　OR ＿＿＿＿＿＿＿＿＿＿

(10). What is　　　　　→ ＿＿＿＿＿＿＿＿＿＿

〈정답과 해설 2P〉

〈정답과 해설 2P〉

1. 다음을 축약형으로 쓰시오. 또 고칠 수 없는 것을 고르시오.

01. I am   → _____

02. He is   → _____

03. She is   → _____

04. It is   → _____

05. That is   → _____

06. We are   → _____

07. You are   → _____

08. They are   → _____

09. We will   → _____

10. I would like → _____

11. I had better → _____

12. I have   → _____

13. We have   → _____

14. They have   → _____

15. He has   → _____

16. There are   → _____

17. How is   → _____

18. This is   → _____

〈정답과 해설 2P〉

2. 다음을 축약형으로 쓰시오. 2가지가 가능한 것은 두 가지를 쓰시오.

01. I am not　　　　　→ _____

02. He is not　　　　 → _____ OR _____

03. She is not　　　　→ _____ OR _____

04. It is not　　　　　→ _____ OR _____

05. We are not　　　　→ _____ OR _____

06. You are not　　　 → _____ OR _____

07. They are not　　　→ _____ OR _____

08. I do not study　　 → _____

09. You can not study　→ _____

10. We should not study → _____

11. I have got the car　→ _____

12. He does not study　→ _____

13. She has not studied → _____ OR _____

14. You have not studied → _____ OR _____

15. They did not play　 → _____

16. You must not play　→ _____

17. We could not play　→ _____

18. They will not play　→ _____ OR _____

〈정답과 해설 2P〉

19. He had not play → _____ OR _____

20. She would not play → _____

memo.

Chapter

02

Number & Unit
수와 단위

Study 01 기수와 서수

기수는 one, two, three … 등 갯수를 나타내는 말이고, 서수는 first, second, third … 등 순서를 나타내는 말이다.
서수는 1(first), 2(second), 3(third)을 제외하고는 기수 끝에 –th를 붙인다.

다만 주의해야할 철자 중에 서수 중 5, 9, 11은 조금 변형이 생겨 fifth, ninth, twelfth가 되며 또 끝에 –t로 끝나는 8 즉 eight은 –h만 붙여서 eighth가 된다. 20, 30, 40, 50...등에서 –ty에서 y가 –ie로 바뀌고 –th를 붙여서 twentieth, thirtieth, fortieth, fiftieth가 된다. 또 4가 four인데 40은 철자u가 없는 forty이다.

기수				서수		
1	–	one		1st	–	first
2	–	two		2nd	–	second
3	–	three		3rd	–	third
4	–	four		4th	–	★fourth

5	–	five	5th	–	★**fifth**
6	–	six	6th	–	sixth
7	–	seven	7th	–	seventh
8	–	eight	8th	–	★**eighth**
9	–	nine	9th	–	★**ninth**
10	–	ten	10th	–	tenth
11	–	eleven	11th	–	eleventh
12	–	twelve	12th	–	★**twelfth**
13	–	thirteen	13th	–	thirteenth
14	–	fourteen	14th	–	fourteenth
15	–	fifteen	15th	–	fifteenth
16	–	sixteen	16th	–	sixteenth
17	–	seventeen	17th	–	seventeenth
18	–	★**eighteen**	18th	–	★**eighteenth**
19	–	★**nineteen**	19th	–	★**nineteenth**
20	–	twenty	20th	–	★**twentieth**
21	–	twenty-one	21st	–	twenty-first
22	–	twenty-two	22nd	–	twenty-second
23	–	twenty-three	23rd	–	twenty-third
24	–	twenty-four	24th	–	twenty-fourth

25	–	twenty-five	25th	–	★twenty-fifth
26	–	twenty-six	26th	–	twenty-sixth
27	–	twenty-seven	27th	–	twenty-seventh
28	–	twenty-eight	28th	–	★twenty-eighth
29	–	twenty-nine	29th	–	★twenty-ninth
30	–	thirty	30th	–	★thirtieth
40	–	★forty	40th	–	★fortieth
50	–	fifty	50th	–	★fiftieth
60	–	sixty	60th	–	★sixtieth
70	–	seventy	70th	–	★seventieth
80	–	★eighty	80th	–	★eightieth
90	–	★ninety	90th	–	★ninetieth

hundred(백)

1,000,000,000,000

trillion(조)   billion(10억)   million(100만)   thousand(천)

다만 아래에서 one은 생략할 수 있다.

100 – (one) hundred

200 – two hundred

1,000 – (one) thousand

10,000 – ten thousand

100,000 – (one) hundred thousand

100th – (one) hundredth

200th – two hundredth

1,000th – (one) thousandth

10,000th – ten thousandth

100,000th – (one) hundred thousandth

1,000,000 – (one) million	1,000,000th – (one) millionth
10,000,000 – ten million	10,000,000th – ten millionth
100,000,000 – (one) hundred million	10,000,000th – (one) hundred millionth
1,000,000,000 – (one) billion	1,000,000,000th – (one) billionth
10,000,000,000 – ten billion	10,000,000,000th – ten billionth
100,000,000,000 – (one) hundred billion	100,000,000,000th – (one) hundred billionth

 확인문제 1

아래 기수와 서수관계이다. 철자가 틀린 것을 찾아 올바로 고치시오.

(01). five – fiveth

(02). four – forth

(03). eight – eightth

(04). nine – nineth

(05). twelve – twelveth

(06). twenty – twentyth

(07). fourty – fourtyth

(08). ninty – nintieth

〈정답과 해설 3P〉

확인문제 2

아래 빈칸의 단위를 영어로 쓰시오.

1,000,000,000,000
(01) (02) (03) (04) |(05)

(01)–

(02)–

(03)–

(04)–

(05)–

〈정답과 해설 3P〉

1. 분수

$$\frac{3}{4}$$

→ 분자는 기수로
→ 분모는 서수로] **three-fourths**
※ 분자와 분모사이에
–(하이픈)을 쓴다.

⊙ 분자는 기수로 분모는 서수로 읽는다. 1일 때 one대신에 a(n)을 많이 쓴다. 다만 1/2는 a half 혹은 one-half를 쓴다.

- $\frac{1}{2}$ a half 혹은 one-half · $\frac{1}{3}$ a third 혹은 one-third

- $\frac{1}{4}$ a fourth, one-fourth 혹은 a quarter

분자가 복수일 때는 분모의 서수 끝에 –s를 붙인다. 보통 분자와 분모사이에 하이픈(–)을 쓴다.

- $\frac{3}{4}$ three-fourths 혹은 three quarters · $\frac{2}{3}$ two-thirds

- $\frac{7}{10}$ seven-tenths · $7\frac{2}{7}$ seven and two-sevenths

2. 소수

⊙ 소수점까지는 기수, 소수점은 point, 소수점 이하는 숫자를 하나씩 순서대로 기수로 읽는다.

- 10.58
  ten, point five eight

- 0. xx 일 때, o(zero)라고 읽거나, point부터 읽는 경우도 많다.
  즉 0.78은
  o(zero), point seven eight
  혹은 point seven eight로 읽는다.

- 4.28
  four, point two eight

- 27.89
  twenty seven, point eight nine

- 89.45
  eighty nine, point four five

- 897.23
  eight hundred ninety seven, point two three

확인문제 3

아래 분수와 소수를 영어로 쓰시오.

(01). $\dfrac{1}{2}$ –

(02). $\dfrac{1}{4}$ –

(03). $\dfrac{1}{5}$ –

(04). $\dfrac{2}{5}$ –

(05). 23.6 –

(06). 523.38 –

〈정답과 해설 3P〉

1. 전화번호

⊙ 전화번호는 한자리씩 읽는다.

- 894-9758

  eight nine four, nine seven five eight
- 956-6549

  nine five six, six five four nine
- 675-8846

  six seven five, eight eight(double eight) four six
- (02) 562-7905

  area code o(zero) two, five six two, seven nine o(zero) five
- (062) 352-9647

  area code o(zero) six two, three five two, nine six four seven
- (041) 342-3978

  area code o(zero) four one, three four two, three nine seven eight

다만 같은 수가 2개 나오면 double이라고 읽을 수 있다.

- (02) 573-3378

    area code o(zero) two, five seven three, three three(double three) seven eight

또 0은 o[ou-오우]라고 읽거나 zero[지어로우]라고도 읽는다.

CF 국제 전화 거는 법

국가번호(country code) – 지역번호(area code) – 전화번호순으로 누른다.

예를 들어

미국국가번호 – 지역번호 – 전화번호

미국(1) – Indianapolis(317) – 전화번호 순으로 누르면 된다.

□ 국제전화 번호

- South Korea 82   – America 미국 1
- Canada 캐나다 1   – China 중국 86
- Japan 일본 81   – Kuwait 쿠웨이트 965
- Thailand 태국 66

 확인문제 4

아래 전화번호를 영어로 쓰시오..

(01). 657-0987 :

(02). (02)785-4532 :

(03). 010-6337-3591 :

(04). (031) 456-7654 :

(05). 81-48-654-9876 :

〈정답과 해설 3P〉

2. 연도와 날짜

① 연도– 연도는 보통 두 자리 씩 끊어 읽는다.

- 1945 – nineteen, forty five
- 1987 – nineteen, eighty seven
- 2017 – twenty, seventeen 혹은 two thousand seventeen

- BC 34 – BC thirty four
- AD 342 – AD three hundred forty two

 확인문제 5

아래 연도를 영어로 읽는 대로 쓰시오.

(01). BC 500 :

(02) AD 372 :

(03) 1919 :

(04) 1945 :

(05) 1960 :

(06) 1997 :

(07) 2015 :

〈정답과 해설 3P〉

② 날짜– 월, 일, 년 순서로 읽는다. the를 붙여 'the 날짜 of 월' 형식으로 읽기도 한다.

  날짜는 순서를 나타내는 말이므로 서수로 읽는다.

- 1960년 4월 19일

    표기: April. 19(th). 1960.

    읽기: April, (the) nineteenth, nineteen sixty

    혹은 the nineteenth of April, nineteen sixty

- 1980년 5월 18일

    표기: May. 18(th). 1980.

    읽기: May, (the) eighteenth, nineteen eighty

    혹은 the eighteenth of May, nineteen eighty

- 2017년 12월 19일

    표기: December. 19(th). 2017.

    읽기: December, (the) nineteenth, twenty seventeen [=two thousand seventeen]

    혹은 the nineteenth of December, twenty seventeen [=two thousand seventeen]

The leader was born on May. 25(th). 2005. [(......) May, (the) twenty fifth, two thousand five(twenty hundred five).]

년도가 없을 때는 월, 일 순서로 읽는다.

또는 the를 붙여 'the 날짜 of 월' 형식으로 읽기도 한다. 날짜는 당연히 서수로 읽는다.

- 1월 30일

    표기: January. 30(th).

    읽기: January, (the) thirtieth 또는 the thirtieth of January

- 5월 9일

    표기: May. 9(th).

    읽기: May, (the) ninth 또는 the ninth of May.

- 12월 24일

　　　표기: December. 24(th).

　　　읽기: December, (the) twenty fourth 또는 the twenty fourth of December

요일과 날짜를 쓸 때는, 요일, 월, 일, 년의 순서로 쓴다.

예를 들어
- 2015년 2월 19일 목요일

　　　표기: Thursday, February. 19(th). 2015

　　　읽기: Thursday, February. (the) nineteenth, twenty fifteen

　　　　= Thursday, the nineteenth of February, twenty fifteen

🔍 확인문제 6

아래 (연)월일을 영어로 표기법과 읽는 법을 쓰시오.

(01). 3월 15일

　　　표기법 : _____

　　　읽는 법 : _____ or _____

(02). 10월 26일

　　　표기법 : _____

　　　읽는 법 : _____ or _____

(03). 12월 12일

　　　표기법 : _____

　　　읽는 법 : _____ or _____

(04). 1945년 8월 15일

　　　표기법 : _____

　　　읽는 법 : _____

　　　　or _____

(05). 1960년 4월 19일

　　　표기법 : _____

　　　읽는 법 : _____

　　　　or _____

〈정답과 해설 3P〉

Level UP

월표시

1월	January	2월	February
3월	March	4월	April
5월	May	6월	June
7월	July	8월	August
9월	September	10월	October
11월	November	12월	December

요일표시

월요일	Monday	화요일	Tuesday
수요일	Wendnesday	목요일	Thurseday
금요일	Friday	토요일	Saturday
일요일	Sunday		

확인문제 7

아래 월을 영어로 쓰시오.

(01). 1월- _____

(02). 2월- _____

(03). 3월- _____

(04). 4월- _____

(05). 5월- _____

(06). 6월- _____

(07). 7월- _____

(08). 8월- _____

(09). 9월- _____

(10). 10월- _____

(11). 11월- _____

(12). 12월- _____

〈정답과 해설 3P〉

확인문제 8

아래 요일을 영어로 쓰시오.

(01). 월요일- _____

(02). 화요일 – _____

(03). 수요일 – _____

(04). 목요일- _____

(05). 금요일 – _____

(06). 토요일 – _____

(07). 일요일- _____

〈정답과 해설 3P〉

1. 먼저 시간을 읽고 분을 기수로 읽는다.

- 6:08 six, o eight
- 6:15 six, fifteen
- 9:30 nine, thirty

◎다만 정각인 경우, 끝에 o'clock을 붙이며 15분은 a quarter, 30분은 half으로 쓰기도 한다.

- 11:00– eleven o'clock
- 12:00– twelve o'clock
- 7:15– seven, fifteen(=a quarter)
- 9:30– nine, thirty(=half)

2. 분을 먼저 쓰는 경우

⊙ after[=past]는 '~를 지나서'다.

- 7:08 – eight after[=past] seven
- 8:15 – fifteen after[=past] eight = a quarter after[=past] eight
- 8:30 – thirty after[=past] eight = half after[=past] eight

⊙ before[=to]는 ' ~전'을 표현한다.

- 9:37– twenty three before[=to] ten
- 10:45– fifteen before[=to] eleven = a quarter before[=to] eleven
- 11:55 – five before[=to] twelve

3. 오전을 말할 때– am을, 오후를 말할 때 pm을 쓴다.

> am : ante meridian
>
> pm : post meridian
>
> (meridian은 라틴어로 정오를 뜻한다. 또한 ante은 '-이전', post는 '-이후'의 뜻이다.)

- am 9:00– am nine o'clock   (오전 아홉시 정각)
- pm 5:20– pm five twenty   (오후 다섯시 20분)

- School begins at 9 o'clock.   학교는 9시 정각에 시작한다.
- Let's meet in the park 7:20.   7시 20분에 공원에서 만나자.
- Fall arrived in Chicago at 12:37 on August 20(th), 2014.

폴은 8월 20일 12시 37분에 시카고에 도착했다.

- They will meet in City Hall square at 10 pm on December 19, 2017.

그들은 2017년 12월 19일 오후 10시에 시청광장에서 만날 것이다.

확인문제 9

아래 시간을 영어로 쓰시오. 시간을 먼저 읽고 분을 읽는 방법(A)과 분을 먼저 읽고 시간을 읽는 방법(B)을 각각 쓰시오.

(01). 1. 2:15분

       A :

       B :

(02). 3:25분

       A :

       B :

(03). 4:30분

       A :

       B :

(04). 5:45분

       A :

       B :

(05). 6:55분

       A :

       B :

(06). 8:27분

       A :

       B :

〈정답과 해설 4P〉

Study **05** 화폐와 온도

1. 화폐

⊙ 먼저 금액을 기수로 읽고 화폐단위를 뒤에 읽는다. 2이상일 때, dollar, euro, fran, pound, ruble은 복수로 읽지만 won, yen, yuan 등은 복수로 읽지 않는다.

- $789– seven hundred eighty nine dollars

달러에서 소수점(.)까지는 dollar, 소수점 이하는 센트(c)이다.

- $56.78– fifty six dollars, seventy eight cents

그냥 소수점은 point로 읽고, 나머지를 읽은 후에 dollar로 읽기도 한다.
즉 위의 $56.78는 fifty six, point seventy eight dollars로 읽을 수 있다.

- ₩50,540 – fifty thousand, five hundred forty won
- ¥45,600– forty five thousand six hundred yen
- €45– forty five euros

₩(원) won	$(달러) dollar
¥(엔) yen	€(유로) euro
元(위안) yuan	

Just 99cents for 12 months ends soon. 12개월 동안 단 99센트가 곧 끝난다.

My elder brother earns $8,000 a year. 나의 형은 연간 8,000달러를 번다.

2. 온도

⊙ 온도의 단위는 섭씨온도(°C)와 화씨온도(°F)가 있다. 숫자를 읽고 ℃는 Celsius, °F는 Fahrenheit로 읽는다.

- 36.5℃(섭씨 36.5도) – thirty six, point five Celsius
- 99℃(섭씨 99도) – ninety nine Celsius
- 911°F(화씨 911도) – nine hundred eleven Fahrenheit

- Normal human body temperature is 36.5~37.1℃. 정상적인 사람 체온은 섭씨 36.5~37.1이다.
- Water boils at 100℃. 물은 100도에서 끓는다.

아래 화폐와 온도를 읽을 때 영어로 쓰시오.

(01). 32℃ :

(02). 897 °F :

(03). $80,000 :

(04). ₩6,550,000 :

(05). ¥500 :

(06). 元545 :

(07). €876 :

〈정답과 해설 4P〉

〈정답과 해설 4P〉

1. 다음을 영어로 쓰시오.

기수	서수
01. 1-	1st-
02. 2-	2nd-
03. 3-	3rd-
04. 4-	4th-
05. 5-	5th-
06. 6-	6th-
07. 7-	7th-
08. 8-	8th-
09. 9-	9th-
10. 10-	10th-
11. 11-	11th-
12. 12-	12th-
13. 13-	13th-
14. 14-	14th-
15. 15-	15th-

〈정답과 해설 4P〉

2. 다음을 영어로 쓰시오.

기수	서수
01. 16–	16th–
02. 17–	17th–
03. 18–	18th–
04. 19–	19th–
05. 20–	20th–
06. 21–	21th–
07. 22–	22th–
08. 23–	23th–
09. 24–	24th–
10. 25–	25th–
11. 26–	26th–
12. 27–	27th–
13. 28–	28th–
14. 29–	29th–
15. 30–	30th–

〈정답과 해설 4P〉

3. 다음을 영어로 쓰시오.

기수	서수
01. 40–	40th–
02. 50–	50th–
03. 60–	60th–
04. 70–	70th–
05. 80–	80th–
06. 90–	90th–
07. 100–	100th–
08. 200–	200th–
09. 1,000–	1,000th–
10. 10,000–	10,000th–
11. 100,000–	100,000th–
12. 1,000,000–	1,000,000th–
13. 10,000,000–	10,000,000th–
14. 100,000,000–	100,000,000th–
15. 1,000,000,000–	1,000,000,000th–
16. 10,000,000,000–	10,000,000,000th–
17. 100,000,000,000–	100,000,000,000th–

18. 256
    기수:
    서수: 256th-

19. 4,563
    기수:
    서수: 4,563th-

20. 87,987
    기수:
    서수: 87,987th-

21. 387,987
    기수:
    서수: 387,987th-

22. 7,987,982
    기수:
    서수: 7,987,982th-

4. 다음 분수와 소수를 영어로 쓰시오.

01. $\dfrac{1}{2}$-

02. $\dfrac{1}{3}$-

03. $\dfrac{1}{4}$-

04. $\dfrac{3}{4}$-

05. $\dfrac{2}{3}$-

06. $\dfrac{1}{5}$-

07. $\dfrac{2}{5}$-

08. $6\dfrac{2}{5}$-

09. $\dfrac{9}{23}$-

〈정답과 해설 5P〉

10. 0.34–

11. 23.76–

12. 4.342–

13. 0.893–

14. 589.765–

15. 3.414–

16. $78 \frac{3}{10}$–

5. 다음 시간을 영어로 읽을 때 표현으로 쓰시오. 시간 분순으로 읽는 방법(A)과 분을 먼저 읽고 시간을 읽는 방법(B)으로 각각 쓰시오.

01. 4:15   (A)–   (B)–

02. 5:30   (A)–   (B)–

03. 6:45   (A)–   (B)–

04. 7:55   (A)–   (B)–

05. 8:08   (A)–   (B)–

06. 9:25   (A)–   (B)–

07. 10:40   (A)–   (B)–

08. 11:00   (A)–   (B)–

09. 11:45   (A)–   (B)–

〈정답과 해설 5P〉

10. 12:17   (A)–   (B)–

6. 다음 전화번호를 영어로 읽을 경우를 영어로 쓰시오.

01. 562-7905 :

02. (02) 573-3581 :

03. (061) 352-9647 :

04. (032) 276-5685 :

05. (041) 888-4532 :

06. 33-2-657-8765 :

07. 82-11-654-4565 :

08. 86-10-876-3423 :

09. 81-70-675-2138 :

10. 86-10-453-5673 :

7. 아래 화폐와 온도를 읽으시오.

01. 632.℃ :

02. 97 ℉ :

03. $80 :

04. ₩76,550 :

05. ¥7,500 :

〈정답과 해설 5~6P〉

06. 元87,545 :

07. €34,876 :

8. 다음 (연)월일을 영어로 표기법과 읽는 법을 쓰시오.

01. 12월 5일
   표기법:
   읽는법:
   혹은

02. 1980년 5월 18일
   표기법:
   읽는 법:
   혹은

03. 1987년 6월 10일
   표기법:
   읽는법:
   혹은

04. 1997년 12월 17일
   표기법:
   읽는 법:
   혹은

05. 2017년 12월 18일
   표기법:
   읽는 법:
   혹은

Chapter

03

Be

Be 동사

Study 01 1형식: ~가 있다.

인칭	수		현재	과거	과거분사
1	단수	I	am	was	been
	복수	we			
2	단수	you(너 한 명)	are	were	
	복수	you(너희들)			
3	단수	he, she, this that, it, a dog	is	was	
	복수	they, these, those, dogs	are	were	

1. 주어 + be + (부사)

- **The fate of democracy** is in youth's hands.
- We struggle for justice, therefore **we are**.
- **They were** in Tokyo last year.

민주주의의 운명이 우리손 안에 있다.

나는 정의를 위하여 투쟁한다. 그러므로 우리는 존재한다.

그들은 작견에 도쿄에 있었다.

2. 'There be ～'와 'Here be～'에서 There나 Here는 주어가 아니고 부사이다.

⊙ There be 주어: '주어가 있다'로 해석

여기에서 쓰인 there는 뜻도 없다. 말을 이끌어내는 there는 부사이다. 동사 뒤에 오는 말이 주어이다.

- There <u>is a bed</u> in Jimmy's room.　　　　　지미의 방에 침대가 있다.
- There <u>were many students</u> in the classroom.　교실에 많은 학생들이 있다.

⊙Here be 주어: '주어가 여기에 있다'로 해석

- Here <u>is your book</u>.　　　　　　　　　너의 책이 여기에 있다.
- Here <u>are many ants</u>.　　　　　　　　많은 개미들이 있다.

There

바보(유도)부사 – there는 아무 뜻이 없다,	거기에 (부사)
'There be동사 등 + 주어'형식으로 쓰인다.	

there는 아무 뜻이 없는 'There is/are + 주어'형식으로 쓰이는 바보(유도)부사와 '거기에'의 뜻으로 쓰이는 경우가 있다. be동사 대신에 live 등의 동사가 쓰일 수 있다.

A. 바보부사: 'There be등 동사 주어'형식으로 쓰인다.

There <u>is some money</u> on the desk.　　　책상위에 많은 돈이 있다.

There <u>are a lot of people</u> on the train.　열차에 많은 사람들이 있다.

There <u>is a movie theater</u> near my house.　나의 집 근처에 영화극장이 있다.

There <u>is a lot of water</u> in the ocean.　　큰 바다에 많은 물이 있다.

There <u>is a car</u> waiting for you.　　　　너를 기다리고 있는 차가 있다.

B. 거기에

I hope we will get <u>there</u> in time.

　　　　　　　　나는 우리가 시간안에 거기에 도착하기를 희망한다.

It took us about six hours to get <u>there</u>.　우리가 거기에 가는데 대략 6시간 걸렸다.

Scotland? I've always wanted to go <u>there</u>.

　　　　　　　　스코틀랜드? 나는 항상 거기에 가기를 원했다.

 **확인문제 1**

다음 문장 중에서 아무 뜻이 없는 바보(유도)부사와 '거기에'라는 뜻 중 하나를 각각 쓰시오.

(01). There is a piano in mom's room.

(02). There are three dogs in the cage.

(03). There is a child in the playground.

(04). There are some ants on the wall.

(05). There is a mosquito on the window.

(06). We will go and play there this weekend.

(07). There are a radio and a smart phone on the desk.

(08). There the boys will play baseball and the girls will draw pictures

〈정답과 해설 6P〉

 확인문제 2

다음 빈칸에 알맞은 be동사의 현재형을 넣어 문장을 완성하시오.

(01). There _____ a bed in George's room.

(02). There _____ three cats on the table.

(03). There _____ a pen and an eraser on the desk.

(04). There _____ children in the playground.

(05). There _____ some books on the desk.

(06). There _____ a window on the wall.

(07). There _____ elephants and monkeys.

(08). There _____ a building in the middle of the pond.

〈정답과 해설 6P〉

 확인문제 3

다음 문장에서 어법상 어색한 문장을 찾아 바르게 고쳐 쓰시오.

(01). There is a piano and a violin in mom's room.

　　　_____ → _____

(02). There are three chickens in the cage.

　　　_____ → _____

(03). There is many children in the playground.

　　　_____ → _____

(04). There are some spiders on the wall.

　　　_____ → _____

(05). There is many people in the theater.

　　　_____ → _____

(06). There are a swimming pool in this hotel.

　　　_____ → _____

〈정답과 해설 6P〉

 확인문제 4

다음 우리말과 같은 의미가 되도록 괄호 안의 단어를 바르게 배열하여 문장을 완성하시오.

(01). 정원에는 많은 나무들이 있다.

　　　(the / trees / of / there / a / in / are / lot / garden).

　　→ _____

(02). 교실에는 학생이 있다.

　　　(student / a / classroom / is / in / there / the).

　　→ _____

(03). 공원에 두 마리의 강아지가 있다. (park, there)

　　→ _____

〈정답과 해설 6P〉

Study 02 2형식: ∼이다.

1. 주어 + be + 명사

- War is the enemy of peace.
- Math is my favorite subject.
- My favorite teacher is my English teacher.
- Laughter is inner jogging.
- Was the man your classmate?

전쟁은 평화의 적이다.
수학은 내가 가장 좋아하는 과목이다.
내가 가장 좋아하는 선생님은 영어선생님이다.
웃음은 마음의 조깅이다.
그 남자가 너의 학급학생이었는가?

2. 주어 + be + 형용사

- The teacher is kind and nice.
- Korean is not easy.
- Science and social study are fun and interesting.

그 선생님은 친절하고 좋으시다.
한국어는 쉽지 않다.
과학은 사회는 재미있고 흥미진진하다.

3. 주어 + be + 전치사 + 명사

- The old book is of value.
- The Korean peninsula is not in peace.

그 오래된 책은 가치 있다.
한반도는 평화로운 상태가 아니다.

확인문제 5

다음 괄호 안에서 알맞은 것을 고르시오.

(01). I [am / are / is] a science teacher.

(02). We [am / are / is] in the conference room.

(03). Seho [am / are / is] a famous actress.

(04). Eric and Mira [am / are / is] soccer players.

(05). This [am / are / is] my cat.

(06). David [am / are / is] happy now.

(07). Jack and Amy [am / are / is] from Canada.

(08). His yellow pencil [am / are / is] on the table.

〈정답과 해설 6P〉

Level UP

be동사가 있는 문장의 의문문과 부정문

A. 의문문
be동사를 주어 앞으로 빼고 문장 끝에 '?'한다. 의문사(덩어리)가 있는 경우 의문사를 맨 앞으로 빼낸다.

We are happy with our school.
→ Are we happy with our school?　　　　우리가 우리학교에 행복한가요?

You are (얼마나) old.
→ How old are you?　　　　몇 살인가?

확인문제 6

다음 문장을 의문문으로 각각 고치시오. 또 의문문을 각각 해석하시오.

(01). There are more subjects to learn.

(02). Your friends are happy with their new school.

(03). They are busy these days with lots of homework.

(04). There were a pencil and an eraser.

(05). Your parents are doing (무엇)

〈정답과 해설 6P〉

B. 부정문
be동사 다음에 not을 쓴다.

My father is very tall.
→ My father is not very tall.

나의 아버지는 매우 크지 않다.

·Everyone is kind to me.
→ Everyone is not kind to me.

모든 사람은 나에게 친절하지 않다.

 확인문제 7

다음 문장을 부정문으로 각각 고치시오.

(01). My friend, Jessica is very cute.

(02). My favorite food was fish.

(03). I and my brother were good cooks.

(04). There are two cats on the table.

〈정답과 해설 7P〉

Plus UP | be동사와 조동사

조동사 다음에는 동사원형을 쓴다. 그래서 '조동사+be'가 된다.

will be	(미래에) ~ 일 것이다.
may be	~ 일지도 모른다.
must be	~ 임에 틀림없다.
can't be	~ 일리 없다.
should be	~ 해야만 한다.

- We should be kind to the elderly.   우리는 노인들에게 친절해야만 한다.
- The patient will be better.   그 환자는 좋아질 것이다.
- My grandfather may be happy.   나의 할아버지는 행복할 수도 있다.
- The policeman must be happy.   그 경찰관은 행복함에 틀림없다.
- The cook can't be happy.   그 요리사는 행복할 리 없다.

조동사 have + been

⊙ 다만 과거에 해당하는 내용일 경우, '조동사+have+p.p(been)'가 된다.

may have been	(과거에) ~ 이었을 지도 모른다.
must have been	(과거에) ~ 이었음에 틀림없다.
can't have been	(과거에) ~ 이었을 리 없다.
should have been	(과거에) ~ 했어야만 했는데.
need not have been	(과거에) ~ 할 필요가 없었는데.

- The teacher may have been kind.   그 선생님은 친절 했을 지도 모른다.
- The teacher must have been kind.   그 선생님은 친절했음에 틀림없다.
- The teacher can't have been kind.   그 선생님은 친절했을 리 없다.
- We should have been kind to customers.   우리는 고객들에게 친절했어야만 했는데.
- We need not have been kind to the thieves.   우리는 그 도둑놈들에게 친절할 필요가 없었는데.

다음 문장을 해석하시오.

(01). The patient will be better.

→ _____

(02). My grandfather may be happy.

→ _____

(03). The policeman must be happy.

→ _____

(04). The cook can't be happy

→ _____

(05). The teacher may have been kind.

→ _____

(06). The teacher must have been kind.

→ _____

(07). The teacher can't have been kind.

→ _____

(08). We should have been kind to customers.

→ _____

(09). We need not have been kind to the thieves.

→ _____

(10). We should be kind to the elderly.

→ _____

〈정답과 해설 7P〉

Grammar in Reading

〈정답과 해설 7P〉

1. 다음 글을 읽고 어법상 어색한 것을 6개 찾아 바르게 고치시오.

Science are my favorite subject. Science not is easy, but they are fun and interesting. My favorite teacher are my math teacher, Miss. Min. She is very kindly and nicely.

01. _____ → _____
02. _____ → _____
03. _____ → _____
04. _____ → _____
05. _____ → _____
06. _____ → _____

2. 다음 글을 읽고 어법상 어색한 것을 4개 찾아 바르게 고치시오.

Hi, My name are Kim Minho. There is four people in my family. They are my father, my mother, my sister, and me. My nickname is Dr. Pet. I love animals and I know a lot about pets. There is three dogs, two cats, and many fish in my house. I'd like to invite your to my house.

01. _____ → _____
02. _____ → _____
03. _____ → _____
04. _____ → _____

3. 위 글의 밑줄 친 ⓐ~ⓔ 중 어법상 어색한 것을 3개 골라 올바로 고치시오.

Middle school ⓐ is not the same as elementary school. We wear a school uniform. There ⓑ is different teachers for each subject. ⓒ We don't stay with our homeroom teacher all day. ⓓ Everything are new to me.

Jiho: I like your school uniform. It's cool.
I: Really? Thanks. ⓔAre your school uniform nice?

정답:
01: _____   02: _____   03: _____

Grammar in Reading

〈정답과 해설 7~8P〉

4. 다음은 Annie와 Jack사이의 웹상 대화문다. 대화문에 들어갈 알맞은 말을 차례대로 쓰시오.

On Web Chatting

Annie: Are you from America?

Jack: No, ⓐ _____ _____. I'm from Canada.

Amy:Oh, I see. ⓑ _____ history your favorite subject?

Jack: No. History ⓒ _____ _____ my favorite. I like math.

Amy: Really? I like math, too. ⓓ _____ reading your hobby?

Jack: Yes.

> • Name: Jack Wright   • Country: Canada
> • Favorite subject: math   • Hobby: reading

01. ⓐ-   02. ⓑ-   03. ⓒ-   04. ⓓ-

5. 다음 (   ) 안에 알맞은 be동사의 현재형을 쓰시오.

There ⓐ (   ) a big tent near the pond. There ⓑ (   ) many national flags around the tent. In front of the tent, a man in black ⓒ (   ) doing a magic show. Two monkeys ⓓ (   ) teasing some children.

01. ⓐ-   02. ⓑ-   03. ⓒ-   04. ⓓ-

6. 다음 (   ) 안에 알맞은 be동사의 현재형을 쓰시오.

Long ago, some people thought that rabbits lived on the moon. Now everyone knows this ⓐ (   ) not true. The moon ⓑ (   ) covered with dry dust. It never rains on the moon. There ⓒ (   ) no living things.

01. ⓐ -   02. ⓑ -   03. ⓒ-

Grammar in Reading

〈정답과 해설 8P〉

7. 아래 글 A와 B에서 쓰인 ⓐ, ⓑ의 There는 서로 다르게 사용된 것이다. 같은 것으로 쓰인 것을 각각 고르시오.

A

ⓐ <u>There</u> are different meanings for waving the hand. When you greet someone, you hold your hand up and move it from side to side. In Europe, however, people wave the hand sideways to say "no." For "good-bye," they raise the palm and wag their fingers up and down.

B

In the Netherlands, people pat one elbow with the palm of the other hand. It means "Don't believe him or her." However, this gesture has a different meanings in Colombia. ⓑ <u>There</u>, it means "You are stingy."

The meanings of gestures are different from culture to culture. When you understand the differences, you will be able to communicate better in other countries.

01. <u>There</u> are many flowers in the picture.
02. Long ago <u>there</u> lived a brave prince.
03. I hope we get <u>there</u> in time.
04. Is <u>there</u> a drugstore around here?
05. How many zebras are <u>there</u> in the zoo?
06. Can you pass me that wine glass <u>there</u>?
07. <u>There</u> are many trees in the picture.
08. <u>There</u> are two people waiting outside.
09. <u>There</u> are many cats in the picture.
10. It took us about six hours to get <u>there</u>.

(01). ⓐ-
(02). ⓑ-

〈정답과 해설 8P〉

1. 다음 괄호 안에서 알맞은 것을 고르시오.

01. (We/He) are from Canada.

02. She (are/is) a math teacher.

03. Jane and Tom (is/are) good friends.

04. Her friend (are/is) in the living room.

05. (Was/Were) you sad?

06. (Is/Are) Ted from England?

07. (Is/Are) these cookies sweet?

08. These bags (is/are) heavy.

09. You and I (am/is/are) thirteen years old.

10. Ms. Smith (was/were) in the library.

2. 다음 문장의 빈칸에 'is' 또는 'are'를 넣어 문장을 완성하시오.

01. _____ there four people in the fourth riddle?

02. There _____ no answer to the fifth riddle.

03. There _____ three riddles for you to solve.

04. _____ there two fathers and two sons?

05. _____ there an island in the lake?

〈정답과 해설 8P〉

06. There _____ a good park near my home.

07. There _____ interesting sites in our city.

08. _____ there a lot of seats in the theater?

09. There _____ some money in my pocket.

10. _____ there apples in the box?

11. _____ there a soccer game today?

12. There _____ some children in the park.

13. There _____ three toys in his room.

14. There _____ water in my ears.

15. There _____ another key in my bag.

16. _____ there no more vibration and no more sound.

17. There _____ a number of other structures around the lighthouse.

3. 다음 문장에서 어법상 어색한 문장을 찾아 바르게 고쳐 쓰시오.

01. There is many people in the theater.

_____ → _____

02. They are in Gwangju last weekend.

_____ → _____

03. My dad and I aren't good at skiing last winter.

_____ → _____

〈정답과 해설 8~9P〉

04. There are a swimming pool in this hotel.

_____ → _____

05. I amn't a basketball player.

_____ → _____

06. Is a dog and a cat under the table?

_____ → _____

07. Is there beautiful flowers in the park.

_____ → _____

08. It is cold yesterday, but it is warm today.

_____ → _____

09. He is 17 years old last year.

_____ → _____

10. Taylor is tall, but he weren't tall last year.

_____ → _____

11. Are there four people in my family?

_____ → _____

12. There are a park near my house.

_____ → _____

13. My cat is sick yesterday afternoon.

_____ → _____

4. 다음 괄호 안에서 알맞은 것을 고르시오.

01. It (is/was) cold yesterday, but it is warm today.

〈정답과 해설 9P〉

02. I (am/was) 15 years old last year.

03. Tom is tall, but he (wasn't/weren't) tall last year.

04. My cat (was/were) sick yesterday afternoon.

05. They (are/were) in Busan last weekend.

06. My sister and I (aren't/weren't) good at skiing last winter.

07. I am a middle school student and my sisters (am/are/is) high school students.

5. 다음 우리말과 같은 의미가 되도록 There를 활용하여 괄호 안의 단어를 활용하여 문장을 완성하시오.

01. 정원에는 많은 나무들이 있다.
(a lot of trees, in the garden).
→ _____

02. 교실에는 학생이 있다.
(a student, in the classroom)
→ _____

03. 공원에 두 마리의 강아지가 있다.
(two dogs, in the park)
→ _____

04. 어항 옆에 고양이가 한 마리 있다.
(the fish bowl, next to, a cat)
→ _____

05. 이 마을에는 오래된 건물들이 있다.
(old buildings, in this town)
→ _____

06. 땅에 눈이 좀 있니?
   (any snow, on the ground)

   → _____

07. 교실에는 몇 명의 학생들이 있다.
   (some, students)

   → _____

08. 테이블 위에 몇 개의 바나나가 있다.
   (bananas)

   → _____

6. 다음 문장을 의문문으로 고치시오.

01. You are gloomy.

   → _____

02. Ted is from England.

   → _____

03. These cookies are sweet.

   → _____

04. There are many pencils on the desk.

   → _____

05. There is a key in the box.

   → _____

06. Jim is taking a piano lesson now.

   → _____

07. They are watering flowers now.

   → _____

〈정답과 해설 9P〉

08. He is a basketball player.

→ _____

09. They are in the library.

→ _____

10. They are farmers.

→ _____

11. The shop is open today.

→ _____

12. You are a good singer.

→ _____

13. They are my socks.

→ _____

14. She is a scientist.

→ _____

15. Crater Lake is in Oregon.

→ _____

16. Today is Constitution Day.

→ _____

7. 다음 문장을 부정문으로 고치시오.

01. You are sad.

→ _____

02. Ted is from England.

→ _____

03. These cookies are sweet.

→ _____

04. There are many pencils on the desk.

→ _____

05. There is a key in the box.

→ _____

06. Jim is taking a piano lesson now.

→ _____

07. They are watering flowers now.

→ _____

08. He is a basketball player.

→ _____

09. They are in the library.

→ _____

10. You are a good singer.

→ _____

11. The shop is open today.

→ _____

12. They are my socks.

→ _____

13. She is a scientist.

→ _____

14. Today is Constitution Day.

→ _____

〈정답과 해설 9P〉

8. 다음 각각의 문장을 과거형으로 고치시오.

01. The actress is gloomy.
→ _____

02. Darius is from Canada.
→ _____

03. Those apples are sour.
→ _____

04. There is much clothing in the cabin.
→ _____

05. There are many books in the library.
→ _____

06. The biologist is taking a lesson now.
→ _____

07. The farmers are watering sweet potatoes now.
→ _____

08. The tall man is a basketball player.
→ _____

09. My son and his friends are in the library.
→ _____

10. The clothing shop is open today.
→ _____

〈정답과 해설 9P〉

9. 다음 문장을 영작하시오.

01. David는 행복하다.

02. David는 행복했다

03. David는 (미래에) 행복할 것이다.

04. David는 행복할 지도 모른다.

05. David는 행복함에 틀림없다.

06. David는 행복할 리 없다.

07. David는 행복했을 지도 모른다.

08. David는 행복했음에 틀림없다.

09. David는 행복했을 리 없다.

10. David는 그 노인들에게 공손했어야만 했는데.(polite, the old)

11. David는 대통령에게 공손할 필요가 없었는데.(polite, president)

12. David는 (과거에서부터 현재까지) 행복하다.

Chapter

04

Basic tense
기본시제

기본시제는 현재, 과거, 미래가 있다.

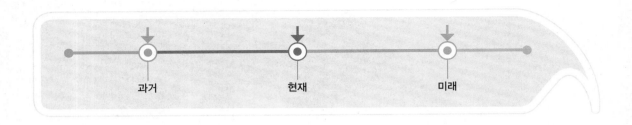

과거   현재   미래

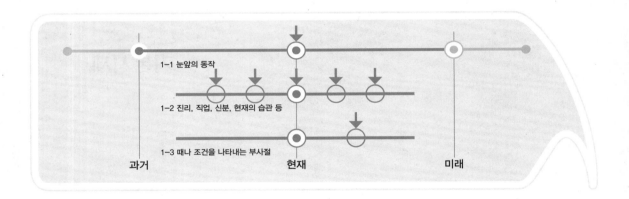

1-1 눈앞의 동작

1-2 진리, 직업, 신분, 현재의 습관 등

1-3 때나 조건을 나타내는 부사절

과거   현재   미래

동사원형/(주어가 3인칭 단수일 때) 동사원형(e)s

⊙ 현재형은 진리, 직업, 신분, 현재의 습관 등일 때 쓴다. **주어가 3인칭 단수일 때는 동사원형에 -(e)s를 붙이고 3인칭 단수를 제외하면'동사원형'을 쓴다. 다만 be동사는 am/are/is 등 특별한 형태를 가진다.**

⊙ 3인칭 단수 제외한 경우 – 동사원형을 쓴다. be동사는 are이다. 다만 I일 때는 am이다.

　• We are very healthy.　　　　　　우리는 매우 건강하다.
　• You are my friends.　　　　　　여러분은 나의 친구들이다.

- The people are farmers in this village.　　　그 사람들은 이 마을 농부들이다.
- The orphans have a book and a pen.　　　그 고아들은 책과 펜을 가지고 있다.
- The volunteers do their duty hard.　　　그 자원 봉사자들은 그들의 의무를 열심히 한다.
- We want to save energy.　　　우리는 에너지를 절약하는 것을 원한다.
- People have five senses.　　　사람들은 5감을 가지고 있다.

◉ 3인칭 단수 – 동사원형(e)s, be동사는 is, have동사는 has, do동사는 does이다.
- The player is very diligent.　　　그 선수는 매우 근면하다.
- The painter has many pictures.　　　그 화가는 많은 그림들을 가지고 있다.
- The architect does his best.　　　그 건축가는 최선을 다한다.
- The sun warms the air up.　　　태양은 공기를 따뜻하게 한다.
- Mother feeds my baby brother everyday.　　　엄마는 나의 아기동생에게 매일 음식을 준다.

 확인문제 1

다음 문장에서 동사의 현재 형태를 쓰시오.

(01). The swimmers (is/are) very tall.

(02). The watermelon (is/are) sweet.

(03). The ocean (has/have) many kinds of fish.

(04). The mountains (has/have) many kinds of plants.

(05). The worker (does/do) his daily work on time.

(06). The young in South Korea (does/do) their military duty.

(07). His attitude (changes/change).

(08). Flowers (opens/open) in spring.

(09). Birds (sings/sing) a song on the tree.

(10). Both students (is/are) equal in age.

(11). Pineapples (grows/grow) on the ground.

(12). The farmer (grows/grow) a crop of potatoes.

(13). My son (brushes/brush) his teeth three times a day.

〈정답과 해설 10P〉

3인칭 단수

1인칭 I와 we, 2인칭 you를 제외한 모든 것이 3인칭이다.

이중 두 개가 아닌 것은 모두 3인칭 단수이다.

this, that, each, either, neither, everyone, it, he, she, the book, this desk, the moon, the sun, a boy, a girl, a man, a deer, a sheep, a fish, a dog, a pig, a computer, a ball, a house, a cat, a pencil, water, voice, sound, food, wood, coffee, fork, beef, cloud, weather, dad, my mother etc.

3인칭 복수

1인칭 I와 we, 2인칭 you를 제외한 모든 것이 3인칭이다.

이중 두 개 이상인 모든 것을 3인칭 복수라고 한다.

both, these, those, the men, women, deer, sheep, people, books, the girls, heaters, clocks, my parents etc.

A. 인칭

인칭이란 1인칭, 2인칭, 3인칭으로 나뉜다. 1인칭에는 하나인 단수 I와 둘 이상인 복수 we가 있다. 그리고 2인칭에는 '너' 하나를 가리키는 단수, '너희들'을 가리키는 복수 you가 같다. 1인칭 I와 we, 단수와 복수의 형태가 같은 2인칭 you를 제외하고는, 사람이든 사물이든 세상의 모든 것은 모두 3인칭이다. 그 중 두 개가 아닌 하나를 '3인칭 단수', 둘 이상을 '3인칭 복수'라 한다.

B. 인칭과 동사

동사	be	do	have	play	teach
3인칭 단수 현재형	is	does	has	plays	teaches
과거형	3인칭 단수와 I일 때 was 나머지일 때 were	did	had	played	taught
3인칭 단수 제외한 현재형	are(I일때 am)	do	have	play	teach

영어에서 3인칭 단수를 나타내는 현재형동사는 특별 취급한다. be동사 일 때 is, do 동사 일 때 does, have동사 일 때 has, 일반 동사 일 때 동사원형에 –(e)s를 붙인다. 과거일 때는 be동사 일 때는 3인칭단수와 I 일 때 was, 나머지는 were를 쓴다. 나머지 동사의 과거형은 3인칭 단수이든 나머지이든 모두 같다.

현재 진행형

am/are/is + 동사원형ing

⊙ 현재 시점에서 진행 중임을 나타낸다. 'am/are/is +동사원형ing'를 쓴다.

- A group is dancing the tango now.   한 그룹이 탱고를 치고 있는 중이다.
- Many people are enjoying the festival.   많은 사람들이 축제를 즐기고 있는 중이다.

 확인문제 2

다음 문장에서 동사의 현재진행 형태를 쓰시오.

(01). Everyone (   ) a great time.(have)

(02). We (   ) in front of Seokguram.(stand)

(03). Mom (   ) the noodles.(cook)

(04). Students (   ) special T–shirts.(sell)

(05). Many people (   ) the festival.(enjoy)

(06). They (   ) different kinds of spaghetti.(enjoy)

(07). The cooks (   ) the vegetable oil in a small pan.(heat)

〈정답과 해설 10P〉

현재형과 현재 진행형

'현재'형은 진리, 직업, 신분, 현재의 습관 등을 나타내지만'현재 진행'형은 현재의 시점에서 일시적으로 진행 중임을 표현한다.

현재

People dance, sing, and play music in the festival.
사람들은 축제에서 춤추고 노래하고 음악을 연주하다.

The next team waits behind the stage in the competition.
다음 팀이 경기를 위해 무대 뒤에서 기다린다.

The parents of the students sell different food from around Asia.
그 학생들의 부모들은 아시아로부터 온 다른 음식들을 판다.

현재진행형

The next team is waiting behind the stage.
다음 팀이 무대 뒤에서 기다리고 있는 중이다.

People are dancing, singing, and playing music.
사람들은 춤추고 노래하고 음악을 연주하고 있는 중이다.

The parents of the students are selling different food from around Asia.
그 학생들의 부모들은 아시아로부터 온 다른 음식들을 팔고 있는 중이다.

Grammar in Reading I

〈정답과 해설 10P〉

1. 아래 내용은 현재의 상황을 설명한 글이다. 동사의 현재형 등 알맞은 동사의 형태를 쓰시오.

What do you ⓐ (do) for your family? You may ⓑ (take) out the garbage. You may clean the house, too. How about friends in other countries? Ben ⓒ (live) in a ranch. In the morning, he ⓓ (become) a little chef for her family. He ⓔ (bake) naan, traditional Indian bread. His family ⓕ (eat) naan with curry. ⓖ (Look) at this! It is ready. His sister says, "Ben, be careful. You may get hurt."

01. ⓐ –   02. ⓑ –   03. ⓒ –
04. ⓓ –   05. ⓔ –   06. ⓕ –
07. ⓖ –

2. 아래 내용은 현재상태의 내용이다. 빈칸에 알맞은 동사의 형태를 쓰시오.

Yuri ⓐ (live) with her mother and grandmother. Her mom usually ⓑ (work) until late. Yuri's grandmother is visiting. Yuri's uncle in Busan today. After school, Yuri ⓒ (ask) her friend, Changmin, "Do you ⓓ (want) to have a snack with me?"
He ⓔ (answer), "I'm sorry. I don't have time."She ⓕ (meet) another friend, Mira. "Do you want to come over for dinner?" "I'm sorry, I can't," says Mira.

01. ⓐ –   02. ⓑ –   03. ⓒ –
04. ⓓ –   05. ⓔ –   06. ⓕ –

3. 다음 내용에서 사용된 동사가 어법상 맞지 않는 것을 있는 대로 찾아 올바로 고치시오.

Petrus is Dutch. He work in the garden. His mother plant tulips. Petrus water the flowers every weekend. He do his best. His mother says, "Petrus, watches out! Don't flood the garden."Katu is from Greenland, Denmark. Dog sledding is a part of his everyday life. His dogs delivers many things to people's houses. Katu guide them from house to house. The lead dog runs in front of the other dogs. Sometimes it runs too fast. Katu says, "Hey! Slow down."

[   ]

Grammar in Reading I

〈정답과 해설 10~11P〉

4. 다음 내용에서 사용된 동사가 어법상 맞지 않는 것을 있는 대로 찾아 올바로 고치시오.

Yuri is sad. In fact, today ⓐ (are) her birthday, but no one ⓑ (remember). There is no seaweed soup and no birthday cake. She ⓒ (gets) home and ⓓ (open) the door. "Surprise!" People ⓔ (jumps) from everywhere in the house. Yuri ⓕ (sees) balloons, gifts, and a cake. Her mother, grandmother, Changmin, Mira, and even her uncle ⓖ (is) there. Yuri just stands there. Her eyes fill up with tears, but on her face, there is a big smile.

01. ⓐ –   02. ⓑ –   03. ⓒ –
04. ⓓ –   05. ⓔ –   06. ⓕ –
07. ⓖ –

5. 다음 (   ) 안의 동사를 현재 진행형으로 고치시오.

On Sunday morning, Hwimin ⓐ (take) a walk. He sees some foreigners. They ⓑ (move) in. A man ⓒ (carry) a desk. He is tall and has curly hair. A woman ⓓ (carry) a chair. She has long hair. Their son ⓔ (hold) something. He has blue eyes. He smiles and talks to Hwimin.

01. ⓐ –   02. ⓑ –   03. ⓒ –
04. ⓓ –   05. ⓔ –

6. 아래 내용은 현재상태의 내용이다. 빈칸에 알맞은 동사의 형태를 쓰시오.

Let's go to the playground first. There people are dancing, singing, and playing music. A group ⓐ (be) dancing the tango now. They ⓑ (be) grandfathers and grandmothers of the students. Wow, they ⓒ (be) great dancers, aren't they?

 Let's go to the back. Oh, the next team ⓓ (be) waiting behind the stage. They are The Rainbow Harmony. The members ⓔ (be) students from different countries. They ⓕ (speak) different languages but sing in great harmony.

01. ⓐ –   02. ⓑ –   03. ⓒ –
04. ⓓ –   05. ⓔ –   06. ⓕ –

Study 02 과거

과거   현재   미래

동사원형(e)d

⊙ 현재 이전, 즉 과거에 일어난 일을 나타낸다. 명백한 과거인 yesterday, last year, 10 days ago, in 1980 등 명백한 과거를 나타내는 말이 있을 때는 반드시 과거를 쓴다. **과거형 동사는 규칙적으로 변화하는 동사는 –(e)d를 붙이다.** 불규칙적으로 변하는 동사는 3단 변화형에서 두 번째인 과거형 동사를 쓴다. be동사의 과거형은 I와 3인칭 단수의 경우 was, 나머지는 were이다.

- The buildings were ancient.   그 빌딩들이 오래 되었다.
- Dad was good at playing the flute.   아빠는 플룻연주를 잘했다.
- Vending machines were everywhere there.   거기에 자판기가 어디에나 있었다.
- Mom cooked fish this morning.   엄마는 오늘 아침에 생선을 요리했다.

 확인문제 3

다음 문장에서 동사의 과거 형태를 쓰시오.

(01). The smart phone (be) his father's.

(02). The travellers in the jewelry (be) Chinese.

(03). The university (be) very famous then.

(04). Two umbrellas (be) in the basket.

(05). You (be) talking to your friend on the phone on our way home.

(06). The early men (have) the skills to catch fish and animals.

(07). The students (go) to the library.

(08). A boy (visit) my office yesterday.

(09). The bad guy (sit) on the floor of his cell.

(10). I (leave) my coat in the spot by the window.

(11). The poor man (have) no money to feed his family.

(12). Many people (begin) to like his painting.

〈정답과 해설 11P〉

Grammar in Reading II

〈정답과 해설 11P〉

1. 다음 빈칸에 동사의 과거형을 쓰시오.

We ⓐ(take) this picture at Cheomseongdae. Isn't it beautiful in the sunset? People in the old days ⓑ (study) the stars in this tower. We ⓒ (take) many pictures from different sides, but it ⓓ (is) the same from every angle. It was really surprising. You must come and see it, too.

01. ⓐ –　　　　　　　　02. ⓑ –　　　　　　　　03. ⓒ –
04. ⓓ –

2. 다음 빈칸에 동사의 과거형을 쓰시오.

It ⓐ(be) a hot summer day. Sleeping Beauty ⓑ (wake) up from a deep sleep. "Cough! Cough! I need some fresh air." She ⓒ (get) out of bed and looked outside.
"Oh, what happened?" She was surprised. "A long time ago, the world ⓓ (be) green and clean. A clean river and many green trees ⓔ (be) around here. Beautiful birds ⓕ (sing) in the fresh air. But the world is now gray and dirty. Birds don't sing any more. Where are the trees? I can't see any trees." She was worried.

01. ⓐ –　　　　　　　　02. ⓑ –　　　　　　　　03. ⓒ –
04. ⓓ –　　　　　　　　05. ⓔ –　　　　　　　　06. ⓕ –

3. 다음 빈칸에 동사의 과거형을 쓰시오.

Beauty ⓐ (think), "The world is dirty. I'm a small girl, but I have to do something. It's not too late. What can I do?"
The next day she ⓑ(meet) her neighbors and ⓒ (ask) for help. They all ⓓ (plant) trees and flowers together. They ⓔ (pick) up the trash around the river and on the streets. Sleeping Beauty ⓕ (is) very tired but happy. "We all have to save the earth. Then the world can become a better place." Her face ⓖ (is) shining with hope.

01. ⓐ –　　　　　　　　02. ⓑ –　　　　　　　　03. ⓒ –
04. ⓓ –　　　　　　　　05. ⓔ –　　　　　　　　06. ⓕ –
07. ⓖ –

Grammar in Reading ll

〈정답과 해설 12P〉

4. 다음 (   ) 안에 알맞은 동사를 쓰시오.

Sejin likes to take pictures. A few weeks ago, Sejin ⓐ (show) his pictures to Yuri. She ⓑ (like) them very much. She wanted to take good pictures, too. She asked Sejin for some advice. He ⓒ (give) three tips to her.

First, ⓓ (hold) the camera at the person's eye level, and then move close to the person.

Second, ⓔ (move) the subject from the center of your picture. You can get a better picture that way.

Third, bright sun can make shadows. Turn your flash on, even in the sunshine. You will get a better picture.

Sejin said, "These tips will be helpful. But they are just tips. Take a lot of pictures. You will learn more on your own."

These days, Yuri ⓕ (go) out every weekend with her camera. She really likes to take pictures. It is her new hobby.

01. ⓐ –

02. ⓑ –

03. ⓒ –

04. ⓓ –

05. ⓔ –

06. ⓕ –

Grammar in Reading II

〈정답과 해설 12P〉

5. 다음 괄호 안에 과거형동사를 어법에 맞추어 쓰시오.

This ⓐ (make) Cupid very angry. "You and your arrows may be bigger," Cupid ⓑ (say), "but I'll show you that my little arrows are more powerful." Cupid ⓒ (shoot) a gold arrow at Apollo. Gold arrows made people fall in love.

Then, Cupid shot a lead arrow at Daphne, the daughter of the river god, Peneus. Lead arrows made people hate others. Daphne was a very beautiful girl who ⓓ (have) long hair and perfect skin. She was very shy, so she lived by herself in the forest.

As soon as Apollo saw Daphne, he fell madly in love with her. He wanted to talk to her, so he came closer to her. But because of Cupid's lead arrow, Daphne hated Apollo. So she ⓔ (run) away as fast as she could. Apollo cried, "Daphne, stop! I love you!" But Daphne ran farther and farther into the forest.

01. ⓐ-   02. ⓑ-   03. ⓒ-
04. ⓓ-   05. ⓔ-

6. 다음 (   ) 안에 주어진 동사의 알맞은 과거형동사를 쓰시오.

Yesterday I ⓐ (take) my nine-year-old sister Yuri to the library. Yuri ⓑ (bring) her iguana with her, but I didn't know about it. The iguana caused a lot of trouble in the library. This morning, Dad ⓒ (tell) Yuri to write an apology letter to Mr. Yun. He told me, "Make sure that her apology is sincere."

Dear Mr. Yun,
My dad wanted me to apologize to you. I am sorry I brought my pet iguana, Tito, to the library in my backpack.

A few days ago, I ⓓ (find) a big green book there. It was full of colorful pictures of iguanas. I wanted to show the book to Tito.

But you said that I could not check out that big green book from the library.
So, I ⓔ (plan) to show it to Tito in the corner. I didn't know that my iguana would cause trouble in the library.

My dad said it was my fault because I brought the iguana to the library. But I think you ⓕ (scare) my iguana first because you screamed and people ran everywhere. Tito didn't scare anyone first.

01. ⓐ-   02. ⓑ-   03. ⓒ-
04. ⓓ-   05. ⓔ-   06. ⓕ-

7. 다음 (   ) 안에 주어진 동사의 알맞은 과거형동사를 쓰시오.

Also, I didn't quite understand the "No Animals" sign on the gate.
To me, it ⓐ (mean) I shouldn't bring big animals like dogs. There ⓑ(be) a picture of a dog on the sign. I didn't know iguanas ⓒ (be) not welcome in the library. Please put up a better sign for kids like me.

Anyway, will you accept my apology? I promise I won't bring Tito to the library again.
I look forward to seeing you soon and telling you, "I'm sorry."

01. ⓐ-   02. ⓑ -   03. ⓒ-

Story 03 미래

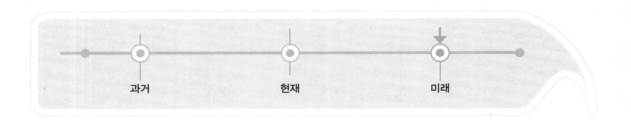

will 동사원형

⊙ 다가올 미래를 나타낼 때, 'will 동사원형'으로 쓴다.

- The teacher will go to the book center.　그 선생님은 북센터에 갈 것이다.
- My daughter will attent the family meeting.　나의 딸은 가족회의에 참여할 것이다.

⊙ 미래를 나타내는 will은 'am/are/is going to 동사원형'으로 쓸 수 있다.

- I will talk about democracy.　　　나는 민주주의에 관해 이야기할 것이다.
  = I'm going to talk about democracy.

 명령문은 '동사원형 ~'
미래를 나타내지만 '~해라'는 명령을 나타내는 경우, '동사원형~'를 쓴다.
Turn your flash on.　　　　　　　　　　너의 전등을 켜라.
Open the windows in your house in the morning.　아침에 너의 집에서 창문을 열어라.

 확인문제 4

다음 문장에서 동사의 미래 형태를 쓰시오.

(01). The world (become) a better place.

(02). Beautiful birds (sing) in the fresh air.

(03). Students (play) baseball next Monday.

(04). Many people (visit) this place and enjoy the beautiful view.

(05). Jones's friend (throw) a surprise party this weekend.

〈정답과 해설 13P〉

Grammar in Reading Ⅲ

〈정답과 해설 13P〉

1. 다음 (   ) 안에 미래형 동사를 쓰시오.

My parents give me 20 dollars for my weekly allowance. Every Sunday I make a plan to spend my money wisely. Here's my plan for next week.

I ⓐ (spend) about 12 dollars on my favorite things – like snacks, movies, and computer games. I often buy small things for my family. I will spend 4 dollars on a hairpin for my mom. She will like it a lot.

I ⓑ (put) 3 dollars in my piggy bank. I save money in a bank, too.

Next year, I ⓒ (buy) the coolest bike with this money. Also I ⓓ (send) 1 dollar to hungry children in Africa. It ⓔ (help) a lot of children.

Does my plan look good? Why don't you make your own?

01. ⓐ –   02. ⓑ –   03. ⓒ –

04. ⓓ –   05. ⓔ –

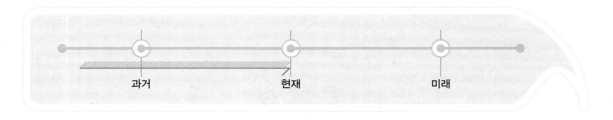

과거   현재   미래

have/ has + p.p: 과거부터~ 현재까지의 구간의 시제를 표현한다.

⊙ 영어에서 현재구간(현재완료)을 나타내는 have/has+p.p는 과거에서부터 현재까지의 구간을 동시에 표현하는 아주 유용한 표현이다.

- My father has worked for the bank for 20 years up to now.
- They have lived in the old cottage for 50 years.
- John has taught earth science in high school since 2000.

나의 아버지는 지금까지 은행에서 일해 왔다.

그들은 50년 동안 그 오두막에서 살고 있다.

존은 2,000년 이후로 지구과학을 가르쳐주고 있다.

확인문제 5

다음 문장에서 동사의 현재구간(완료) 형태를 쓰시오.

(01). He (study) Chinese for 4 years up to now.

(02). They (work) at the factory since 2012.

(03). The boy (meet) his old friends last week.

(04). The writer (write) 10 English text books up to now.

〈정답과 해설 13P〉

further study
경험, 결과, 계속 끝남을 나타내는 현재구간– 'have p.p'

현재구간은 과거에서부터 현재까지의 경험, 결과, 계속, 끝남(완료)[암기법-경결계끝]을 나타낸다.

현재구간

① 경험– before, ever, never, sometimes, 몇 번(once ~ times), often와 함께 쓰인다.
- My sister has once been to Hawaii.　　　　　나의 누이는 하와이에 가본 적이 있다.
- I have driven my dad's car two times.　　　　나는 나의 아빠의 차를 두 번 운전해 본 적이 있다.

② 결과– 보통 leave, go, come, lose, buy 등의 동사가 have gone/come/lost/bought등으로 쓰일 경우　　[암기법– 떠나(leave)면서 가다(go)가 산(buy) 우산을 오다(come)가 잃어버렸다(lose).]
- Simon has already sold his car.　　　　Simon은 이미 그의 차를 팔았다.
- Ms. Lee has lost her bag.　　　　Ms. Lee는 그녀의 가방을 잃어버렸다.
- My mom had bought the book.　　　　나의 엄마가 책을 샀다.

③ 계속– for, since와 함께 쓰인다.
- Chris Kim have played soccer in the club since 2012.

　　　　　　　　　　Chris Kim은 2012년 이후로 그 클럽에서 축구를 하고 있다.

④ 완료(끝남)– already, now, yet, just
- Mom has arrived now.　　　　엄마는 지금 도착했다.
- My husband has gone to his home town.　　　　나의 남편이 그의 고향에 가버렸다.

CF　have been to와 have gone to

have been to는 경험과 끝남을 나타내고 have gone to는 결과를 나타낸다.

– have been to

① 경험
- They have never been to New York.　　　그들은 결코 뉴욕에 가본 적이 없다.

② 끝남
- My children have been to the airport to see my wife off.

나의 아이들은 나의 아내를 환송하기 위하여 공항에 갔다가 왔다.

– have gone to (결과)
- My son has gone to Paris.　　　나의 아들은 파리에 가버렸다. (그래서 여기에 없다.)

 확인문제 6

다음 문장은 과거에서부터 현재까지의 경험, 결과, 계속, 끝남을 나타내는 현재구간(현재완료)형태의 문장들이다. 경험, 결과, 계속, 끝남(완료) 중 하나를 쓰시오.

(01). I have never played baseball.

(02). Have you ever seen a lion?

(03). Spring has come now.

(04). The writer has written a novel for 30 years.

(05). The man has lived in Seoul since 1999.

(06). The travellers have gone to China for their holidays.

(07). Sally has been to London five times.

(08). Mark has lost his cell phone.

(09). He has finished his homework now.

(10). My mother has taught science at the high school for 15 years.

〈정답과 해설 13P〉

〈정답과 해설 13~14P〉

1. 다음 각 문장에서 주어 They 등의 주어를 모두 He로 바꿔 문장을 올바로 쓰시오.

01. They pass the narrow lane.

→

02. The Korean youths do the military duty.

→

03. The boys finish their task on time.

→

04. They play the drum in the concert

→

05. They watch baseball on TV.

→

06. They study social relationship.

→

07. They have a large house.

→

08. The children want some cookies.

→

09. Jane and Tony use the phone in class.

→

10. My friends study English hard.

→

11. The people say that the president is a dictator.

→

12. Hana and her brother visit their aunt every Sunday.

→

〈정답과 해설 14P〉

13. The neighbors want to buy a big house to live in.
    →

14. My daughters arrive in London.
    →

2. 다음 문장을 주어진 주어로 시작하는 문장으로 바꿔 쓰시오.

01. The students go to school by bus.
    → The student _____

02. The children watch TV a lot.
    → The child _____

03. My friends make some cookies.
    → My friend _____

04. My sisters visit their aunt every Sunday.
    → My sister _____

05. His brothers get up late on Sundays.
    → His brother _____

06. My brother and sister wash the dishes.
    → My sister _____

07. My parents have a notebook computer.
    → My dad _____

08. Yuri and her brother study until late at night every day.
    → Yuri _____

09. The Jacksons go with their son there.
    → Jackson _____

10. Farmers sow the seeds in the field.

→ A farmer _____

3. 다음 문장 중에서 어법상 맞지 않는 것을 찾아 올바로 고치시오.

01. My friend make some cookies.

→

02. My sister visit her aunt every Sunday.

→

03. His brother gets up late on Sundays.

→

04. Hans wash the dishes.

→

05. My dad have a notebook computer.

→

06. Yuri study until late at night every day.

→

07. There Jackson goes with his son.

→

08. They needs your help.

→

09. John and his sister has black eyes.

→

10. My uncle teachs Korean at a middle school.

→

〈정답과 해설 14P〉

11. Yesterday was his birthday. We bought a T-shirt for him.
→

12. The nurse usually skip breakfast, but this morning she ate it.
→

13. The doctor goes to bed early because he was very tired.
→

14. My grandma has come to my birthday party yesterday.
→

15. The father were both the son of the grandfather and the father of the grandson.
→

4. 다음 문장에서 어법상 맞지 않는 것을 찾아서 올바로 고치시오. 틀린 것이 없는 문장은 '맞음'으로 표시하시오.

01. The tiger eat grass.
→

02. Jane ride her bike.
→

03. Some birds flies in the sky.
→

04. His horse's name is Friday.
→

05. They eats only three eggs.
→

06. Each person have one egg.
→

〈정답과 해설 14P〉

07. Are you interested in sports?

→

08. How is that possible?

→

09. What is your favorite subject?

→

10. What sports is you interested in?

→

11. They all eats eggs every morning.

→

12. There are two fathers and two sons.

→

13. A man ride into a town on Friday.

→

14. Are you interested in these riddles?

→

15. Can he thinks of any other riddles?

→

16. Jeniffer can shares them with your friends.

→

17. My grandfather doesn't has breakfast.

→

18. Do my grandfather have breakfast?

→

19. The girl's brother wear the size large.

→

20. The man shows some large sweaters.

    →

5. 다음 밑줄 친 곳에 알맞은 동사의 과거형을 빈칸에 쓰시오.

01. The tiger _____ grass. (eat)

02. Jimmy _____ her bike. (ride)

03. Some birds _____ in the sky. (fly)

04. Kevin and I _____ to the library last Friday. (go)

05. She _____ Chris at Amy's birthday party yesterday. (meet)

06. My grandfather _____ this house in 1978. (build)

07. Yesterday was Minho's birthday. We _____ a book for him. (buy)

08. The movie _____ an hour ago. (start)

09. They _____ their uncle's house last Saturday. (visit)

10. My grandma _____ to my birthday party three days ago. (come)

11. John _____ some comic books yesterday. (read)

12. Mike and I _____ baseball last Sunday. (play)

13. My father _____ the house in 1999. (build)

14. It _____ to rain last night. (begin)

15. Seho _____ this novel a month ago. (read)

〈정답과 해설 14P〉

16. She _____ her lost wallet yesterday. (find)

17. Mina _____ an interesting novel in 2000. (write)

18. Seho _____ English yesterday. (study)

19. Nara _____ in front of a painting then. (stop)

20. We _____ our bike in the park two weeks ago. (ride)

6. 다음 문장을 괄호 안에 있는 단어를 활용하여 문장을 영어로 쓰시오.
(필요시 주어진 단어를 변형하여 사용하시오.)

01. 그 소녀는 그녀의 오빠를 위한 스웨터를 원한다. (a sweater)
→

02. 그 소년은 그의 누이의 키를 모른다. (height)
→

03. 두 아버지들과 두 아들들이 오직 세 개의 알을 먹는다. (eat)
→

04. 그 남자는 Friday라고 이름 불리는 그의 말을 탔다. (ride)
→

05. 그 작가는 수수께끼가 재미있다고 생각지 않는다. (riddles)
→

06. 온도가 때때로 내려간다. (Temperature, from time to time)
→

07. 가격이 때때로 올라간다. (price)
→

〈정답과 해설 14~15P〉

08. 그 여자는 2012년에 좋은 소설을 썼다. (write)

→

09. 그 남자는 다음 주 도시를 떠날 것이다. (leave)

→

10. 대통령이 서울에 내일 도착하여 금요일에 뉴욕을 향하여 떠날 것이다. (president. leave for)

→

7. 다음 문장에서 틀린 것을 총 12개를 찾아 올바로 고치시오.

Maria is learning sign language. Today her class is on a field trip to a concert.
There is big and small drums on the stage. There are also a young woman on the stage.

"She have no shoe on!" Maria say. The teacher smile and say, "She is deaf. She feels the music through her feet."The drummer strikes her drums.

Then the concert begins. Maria takes off her shoes. She wants to feel the music better. Maria like the drummer and the music. She love the concert. The concert is over, and the students meet the drummer.

"I am very ill when I was seven," sign Ms. Ellis, "And I lose my hearing.""What did you do then?" signs Maria."I really wanted be with others," Ms. Ellis signs.
"Music is such a wonderful language!"

01.	02.
03.	04.
05.	06.
07.	08.
09.	10.
11.	12.

Chapter

05

Negative & Question Sentence
부정문과 의문문

Study 01 부정문

1. 부정문 만드는 법

Pattern 1- be동사/조동사가 있는 경우	Pattern 2- be동사/조동사가 없는 경우
be동사/조동사 not	do/does/did not 동사원형

be동사/조동사 있는 경우

⊙ be동사나 조동사 다음에 not만 쓰면 된다.

- Life is a journey.
  - → Life is not a journey.

  인생은 여행이다.

- Laughter is the best medicine.
  - → Laughter is not the best medicine.

  웃음은 가장 좋은 약이다.

- Autumn breeze was blowing softly.
  - → Autumn breeze was not blowing softly.

  가을 산들바람이 부드럽게 불고 있는 중이다.

- President will attend the meeting.
  - → President will not attend the meeting.

  대통령이 회의에 참가 할 것이다.

- The singer can dance on the big stage.
  - → The singer can not dance on the big stage.

  그 가수는 큰 무대에서 춤 출수 있다.

- The dancer may go to the banquet.
  - → The dancer may not go to the banquet.

  그 댄서는 연회에 갈 것이다.

- You should interfere in other's private concerns.
  - → You should not interfere in other's private concerns.

  너는 다른 사람의 개인 일에 간섭해야만 한다.

- The players ought to comply with the game rules.
  - → The players ought not to comply with the game rules.

  그 선수들은 게임의 룰을 따라야 만 한다.

- We have been waiting for this moment for a long time.
  - → →We have not been waiting for this moment for a long time.

  우리는 오래 동안 이 순간을 기다리고 있는 중이다.

확인문제 1

다음 각 문제를 부정문으로 고치시오.

(01). Bees are flying insects.

　→

(02). Beer is the world's alcoholic beverage.

　→

(03). All the medicine is poison.

　→

(04). Beer bottle is made of glass.

　→

(05). The officials were corrupt.

　→

(06). Excess weight can decrease your good cholesterol.

　→

(07). You should chew gum in public.

　→

(08). Muammar Qaddafi has been killed.

　→

(09). The minister will reach the construction site.

　→

(10). The ambulance driver will arrive at the hospital soon.

　→

〈정답과 해설 15P〉

be동사나 조동사가 없이 일반동사만 오는 경우

⊙ 일반동사 앞에 not을 쓰고 not앞에 do-does-did를 쓴다.

① 일반동사 원형일 때 (주어가 3인칭단수가 아닌 현재일 때) – do not(=don't) 동사원형

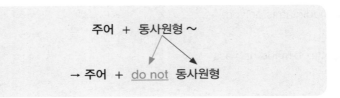

- The roses smell sweet.   장미꽃들이 달콤한 향기가 난다.
  → The roses do not(=don't) smell sweet.
- Children like something sweet.   아이들은 달콤한 어떤 것을 좋아한다.
  → Children do not(=don't) like something sweet.
- Most young people want something funny   대부분의 젊은 사람들은 재미있는 무엇인가를 한한다.
  → Most young people do not(=don't) want something funny.

② 일반동사(e)s 일 때 (주어가 3인칭단수이고 현재일 때) – does not(=doesn't) 동사원형
3인칭단수 현재 표시는 does가 하고 있으므로 반드시 동사원형을 쓴다.

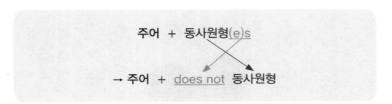

- Everything goes well.   모든 것이 잘되고 있다.
  → Everything does not(=doesn't) go well.
- This cookie tastes good.   이 쿠키 맛이 좋다.
  → This cookie does not(=doesn't) taste good

③ 일반동사의 과거형 때 – 주어 + did not 동사원형

did not(=didn't) 동사원형– 과거 표시는 did가 하고 있으므로 동사는 반드시 동사원형을 쓴다.

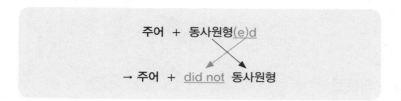

- We drove slowly by an elementary school.   우리는 초등학교까지 천천히 운전했다.
  - → We did not (=didn't) drive slowly by an elementary school.
- Their stories sounded so unbelievable at the time 그들의 이야기는 그 때에 너무나 믿을 수 없게 들렸다.
  - → Their stories did not(=didn't) sound so unbelievable at the time.

 확인문제 2

다음 문장의 부정문을 각각 쓰시오.

(01). Koreans use both spoons and chopsticks.

 →

(02). My parents want me to have a girl friend.

 →

(03). Thousands of residents rely on the city's buses and street cars.

 →

(04). In deserts, it rains less than 300 mm a year.

 →

(05). This green roof keeps the building cooler in summer.

 →

(06). Some girls stood in line for several hours.

 →

(07). Herby's left ankle remained pinned under a fallen beam.

 →

(08). A rescue team from Miami arrived early Friday morning.

 →

(09). The South Korea soccer team can defeat that of Japan

 →

(10). Jisu and Minho decided to go shopping at the thrift shop.

 →

〈정답과 해설 15P〉

Study 02 의문문

1. 의문사가 없는 의문문

의문사 없는 의문문; 형태별

Pattern 1. be동사나 조동사가 있는 경우

주어 + be동사/조동사 + (일반동사) ~

→ be동사/조동사 + 주어 + (일반동사) ~?

Pattern 2. 일반동사원형 – 3인칭 단수를 제외한 현재형

주어 + (일반동사원형) ~

→ Do + 주어 + (일반동사원형) ~?

Pattern 3. 동사원형(e)s– 일반동사의 3인칭 단수 현재형

주어 + 일반동사원형(e)s ~

→ Does + 주어 + 일반동사원형 ~?

Pattern 4. 동사원형(e)d 등 과거형

주어 + 일반동사원형(e)d ~

→ Did + 주어 + 동사원형 ~?

be동사/조동사 있는 의문문

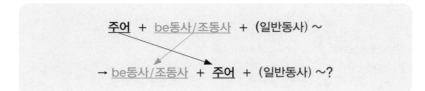

주어 + be동사/조동사 + (일반동사) ~

→ be동사/조동사 + 주어 + (일반동사) ~?

- You are disappointed with your grades.
  - → Are you disappointed with your grades?   너는 너의 학점에 실망스럽냐?
- She was very surprised to hear the news.
  - → Was she very surprised to hear the news?   그녀는 그 뉴스를 듣고 매우 놀랬는가?
- No one can live without air and water.
  - → Can no one live without air and water?   아무도 공기와 물 없이 살 수 없는가?
- We could no longer see the actor.
  - → Could we no longer see the actor?   우리는 더 이상 그 배우를 볼 수 없는가?
- A psychiatrist can help people find possible solutions.
  - → Can a psychiatrist help people find possible solutions?

정신과 의사는 사람들이 가능한 해결책을 찾도록 도울 수 있는가?

 확인문제 3

다음 각 문제에서 각각 의문문으로 고치시오.

(01). You may think I'm lonely.

　→

(02). Meditation can also improve concentration.

　→

(03). This is the house in which she lives.

　→

(04). A small community is called a town.

　→

(05). The woman was clearing the table.

　→

(06). I must bring you the umbrella.

　→

(07). You can speak any foreign languages.

　→

(05). The woman was clearing the table.

　→

(06). I must bring you the umbrella.

　→

(07). You can speak any foreign languages.

　→

(08). You have ever thought about a life.

　→

(09). The man is putting some flowers on the table.

　→

(10). There are many different kinds of communities.

　→

(11). You can tell me where the post office is.

　→

(12). Jongsu may develop a computer program in the future.

　→

〈정답과 해설 16P〉

be동사/조동사 없는 일반동사 있는 의문문

① 일반동사가 동사원형인 경우 (주어가 3인칭단수가 아닌 현재인 경우)

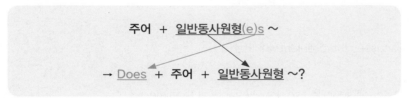

- You have no idea.
  - → Do you have no ideas?　　　　　　　　너는 알지 못하는가?
- Children like something sweet.
  - → Do Children like something sweet?　　아이들이 달콤한 무엇을 좋아한가?

② 일반동사가 동사원형(e)s (주어가 3인칭단수이면서 현재인 경우)

: does가 3인칭 단수표시하고 있기 때문에 반드시 동사원형을 쓴다.

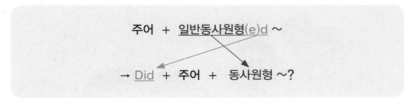

- The sun gives us passion.
  - → Does the sun give us passion?　　　태양은 우리에게 열정을 주는가?
- The silk scarf feels smooth.
  - → Does the silk scarf feel smooth?　　그 실크 스카프가 부드럽게 느껴진다.

② 일반동사가 과거인 경우 : did가 과거 표시하고 있기 때문에 동사는 반드시 동사원형을 쓴다.

주어 + 일반동사원형(e)d ~

→ Did + 주어 + 동사원형 ~?

- You heard what I said.
  - → Did you hear what I said?　　　　　너는 내가 말한 것을 들었는가?
- Each pot needed a different sign.
  - → Did each pot need a different sign?　각각의 단지들은 다른 표시가 필요했는가?

다음 문장을 의문문으로 고치시오.

(01). These cookies smell delicious.

    →

(02). You remember me.

    →

(03). They depend to each other.

    →

(04). You know what you want to be.

    →

(05). They help you meet your basic needs.

    →

(06). Mike decides to come back home.

    →

(07). Ann buys some cloths to make a dress.

    →

(08). He discusses the problem with her.

    →

(09). Their stories sounded so unbelievable at the time.

    →

(10). Tom wanted me not to play the piano at night.

    →

(11). The doctor advised me to exercise regularly.

    →

〈정답과 해설 16P〉

have동사

have동사는 일반동사와 조동사적 성격으로 각각 쓰인다.

A. 일반동사

have는 일반동사로 '가지다'라는 뜻의 3형식과 'have + 목적어 + 동사원형/p.p'형식의 5형식으로 '목적어가 ～하게 하다(～ 상태가 되다)'로 쓰인다.

(3형식) We have a good room. 우리는 좋은 방을 가지고 있다.

(5형식) Dad has me clean my room. 아빠는 내가 나의 방을 청소하게 했다.

일반동사 일 때는 do-does-did를 써서 부정문과 의문문을 만든다.

He has a good car. 그는 좋은 차를 가지고 있다.

부정문 → He doesn't have a good car.

의문문 → Does he have a good car?

We have much money. 우리는 많은 돈을 가지고 있다.

부정문 → We don't have much money.

의문문 → Do we have much money?

B. 조동사적 성격(have/has/had+p.p)

'have+p.p'에서 have는 조동사처럼 쓰인 것으로 have다음에 not을 써서 부정문을 만든다.
또 have를 주어 앞으로 빼서 의문문을 만든다.

They have lived in Seoul. 그들은 (과거에서 현재가지) 서울에서 살고 있다.

부정문 → They have not lived in Seoul.

의문문 → Have they lived in Seoul?

The man has studied Chinese for 10 years. 그 남자는 10년 동안 중국어를 공부하고 있다.

부정문 → The man has not studied Chinese for 10 years.

의문문 → Has the man studied Chinese for 10 years?

다음 문장을 부정문과 의문문으로 각각 고치시오.

(01). You have a magazine to read.

　　　부정문:

　　　의문문:

(02). He has a handsome boy.

　　　부정문:

　　　의문문:

(03). The boy has played the flute.

　　　부정문:

　　　의문문:

(04). They have worked in the bank.

　　　부정문:

　　　의문문:

〈정답과 해설 16P〉

2. 의문사 있는 의문문 만들기

의문사 있는 의문문; 형태별

의문사 있는 의문문은 의문사 없는 의문문만드는 방법과 같이 be동사나 조동사가 있으면 be동사나 조동사를 앞으로 빼고, be동사나 조동사가 없는 일반동사이면 do-does-did를 앞에 쓰고 동사는 반드시 원형을 쓴 다음 문장 끝에 '?'한다. 그런 다음 의문사(덩어리)를 맨 앞에 써준다.

Pattern 1. be동사나 조동사가 있는 경우

주어 + <u>be동사/조동사</u> + (일반동사) ~ <u>의문사 덩어리</u>

→ <u>의문사 덩어리</u> + <u>be동사/조동사</u> + 주어 + (일반동사) ~?

Pattern 2. 일반동사원형 – 3인칭 단수를 제외한 현재형

주어 + <u>(일반동사원형)</u> ~ <u>의문사 덩어리</u>

→ <u>의문사 덩어리</u> + <u>do</u> + 주어 + (일반동사원형) ~?

Pattern 3. 동사원형(e)s– 일반동사의 3인칭 단수 현재형

주어 + <u>일반동사원형(e)s</u> ~ <u>의문사 덩어리</u>

→ <u>의문사 덩어리</u> + <u>does</u> + 주어 + <u>일반동사원형</u> ~?

Pattern 4. 동사원형(e)d 등 과거형

주어 + <u>일반동사원형(e)d</u> ~ <u>의문사 덩어리</u>

→ <u>의문사 덩어리</u> + <u>did</u> + 주어 + <u>동사원형</u> ~?

be동사나 조동사가 있는 경우

주어 + <u>be동사/조동사</u> + (일반동사) ~ <u>의문사 덩어리</u>

→ <u>의문사 덩어리</u> + <u>be동사/조동사</u> + 주어 + (일반동사) ~?

- The couple are fighting each other 왜.
  - → Why are the couple fighting each other?　　　왜 그 커플들은 싸우고 있나요?
- Mother Teresa was born 어디에서.
  - → Where was Mother Teresa born?　　　어디에서 마더 테라사가 태어났나요?
- We should do 무엇.
  - → What should we do?　　　우리가 무엇을 해야 하나요?
- The people have lighted a candle 왜.
  - → Why have the people lighted a candle?　　　왜 국민들은 촛불을 켜나요?
- You would like 얼마나 많은 **tickets**.
  - → How many tickets would you like?　　　얼마나 많은 티켓이 필요하나요?
- It is from here to the bus stop 얼마나 멀리.
  - → How far is it from here to the bus stop?　　　여기에서 버스 정거장 까지 얼마나 먼가요?

be동사나 조동사가 없는 일반동사인 경우

① 3인칭 단수 현재인 경우

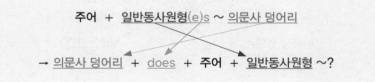

주어 + <u>일반동사원형(e)s</u> ~ 의문사 덩어리

→ <u>의문사 덩어리</u> + <u>does</u> + 주어 + <u>일반동사원형</u> ~?

- He lights a candle 왜.
  - → Why does he light a candle?　　　그는 왜 촛불을 켜나요?
- The novelist writes adventuresome novels 어디에서.
  - → Where does the novelist write adventuresome novels?　　　그 소설가는 어디에서 모험소설을 쓰나요?
- The anthropologist explores the remains 언제.
  - → When does the anthropologist explore the remains?　　　그 인류학자는 유적지를 언제 탐험하나요?

② 3인칭 단수를 제외한 현재인 경우

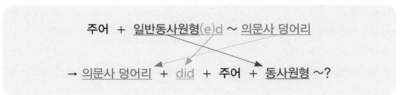

주어 + (일반동사원형) ~ 의문사 덩어리

→ 의문사 덩어리 + do + 주어 + (일반동사원형) ~?

- Your friends help the elderly to do 무엇.
    - → What do your friends help the elderly to do?   너의 친구들은 그 노인들이 무엇을 하도록 돕나요?
- The players exercise 어디.
    - → Where do the players exercise?   그 선수들은 어디에서 운동하나요?
- They obey their parents 어떻게.
    - → How do they obey their parents?   그들은 그들의 부모님을 어떻게 복종하나요?

③ 과거인 경우

주어 + 일반동사원형(e)d ~ 의문사 덩어리

→ 의문사 덩어리 + did + 주어 + 동사원형 ~?

- The people lighted a candle 왜.
    - → Why did the people light a candle?   왜 국민들은 촛불을 켰나요?
- Her father passed away 언제.
    - → When did her father pass away?   언제 그녀의 아버지가 돌아 가셨어요?
- Albert Einstein sought for 무엇.
    - → What did Albert Einstein seek for?   Albert Einstein은 무엇을 추구하였나요?
- You went to your hometown 왜.
    - → Why did you go to your hometown?   너는 너의 고향에 왜 갔어요?

다만, 주어가 의문사일 때

⊙ 주어자리에 의문사 쓰고 끝에 ?만 쓴다.

$$(\;X\;) + \begin{cases} \text{be동사} \\ \text{조동사 + 동사원형} \\ \text{동사원형(e)s} \\ \text{동사원형(ed)} \end{cases} + \begin{matrix} \sim . \\ \sim ? \end{matrix}$$

→ 의문사

- 누구 wants to buy the house.
  → Who wants to buy the house? 　　　　　　누가 그의 집을 사는 것을 원하나요?
- 누구 threw away such a terrific couch.
  → Who threw away such a terrific couch? 　　누가 그렇게 멋진 의자를 내던져 버렸나요?
- 무엇 brought you here.
  → What brought you here? 　　　　　　　무엇이 너를 여기로 데려 왔나요?
- 무엇 is wrong with wearing jeans.
  → What is wrong with wearing jeans? 　　청바지를 입는 것과 관련 무엇이 잘못 되었나요?
- 무엇 happened to the widow's children after the widow died.
  → What happened to the widow's children after the widow died?

　　　　　　　　　　　　　　　　과부가 죽은 후 과부의 아이들에게 무엇일이 일어났나요?

CF　의문사가 형용사인 경우에 명사가, 또 의문사가 부사인 경우는
　　　형용사(+명사) 등이 덩어리 채 함께 앞으로 움직인다.

- He is 얼마나 old.
  → How old is he? 　　　　　　　　그가 몇 살인가요?
- She has 얼마나 많은 books.
  → How many books does she have? 　그녀가 얼마나 많은 책을 가지고 있어요?
- You like 어떠한 종류의 books.
  → What kind of books do you like? 　무엇이 너를 여기로 데려 왔나요?

 **확인문제 6**

다음 괄호 안에서 알맞은 것을 고르시오.

(01). (무엇) happened?

→

(02). (누구의) car is this?

→

(03). (어떤) girl is your daughter?

→

(04). (어디) did you lose your dog?

→

(05). (무엇) does my dog look like?

→

(06). (얼마나 먼) is the City Hall from here?

→

(07). (얼마나 많은) tickets would you like?

→

(08). (어디에) is the post office?

→

(09). (무엇) are you doing now?

→

(10). (왜) did you leave NCA?

→

(11). (왜) did you go to those places?

→

(12). (어떠한) is everything going, Mike?

→

(13). (무엇) should we do?

→

(14). (어떠한) was your trip to Paris?

→

(15). (얼마나 자주) does the man play volleyball?

→

(16). (어떠한 것) do you like better?

→

(17). (어떠한) was your weekend?

→

(18). (얼마) is a one-way ticket to Grand Central?

→

〈정답과 해설 16P〉

다음 문장을 의문문으로 고치시오.

(01). You have to meet him 몇 시.

→

(02). Too many cooks spoil the broth 왜.

→

(03). The children play baseball 어디.

→

(04). The schools begin 몇 시.

→

(05). The Korean people light candles 왜

→

(06). You like 어떤 color better, red or green.

→

(07). You lost the baby 어디.

→

(08). Mother Teresa's mother did 무엇 for a living.

→

(09). Mother Teresa became a nun 언제?

→

(10). You went to the shopping center 왜.

→

(11). She looks like 무엇.

→

(12). He went to the palace 어떻게.

→

(13). The bus runs through the city 몇 번 a day.

→

(14). The professor teaches you literature 무슨 요일에.

→

(15). 무엇 is wrong with these turtles.

→

(16). 누구의 face resembles that of a mouse.

→

(17). The man plays volleyball 얼마나 자주.

→

(18). I can pick it up 언제

→

〈정답과 해설 16P〉

further study 의문사의 종류

의문사의 종류– 의문사도 품사에 따라 사용위치가 다르다. 주어, 목적어, 보충어 등에 사용하는 의문대명사, 명사앞과 보충어자리에서 명사 꾸며주는 의문형용사, 동사, 형용사, 다른 부사, 문장전체를 꾸며주는 의문부사가 있다.

의문사품사	의문사		
대명사	who 누구		사람을 나타내며 주어, 목적어, 보충어자리에서 사용
	whom 누구		사람을 나타내며 목적어에 사용. 다만 who로 대신 쓰는 경우가 많다.
	what 무엇		사물을 나타내며 주어, 목적어, 보충어 등에서 사용
	which 어떤 것		사람이나 사물을 나타내며 선택의 대상이 있는 경우 사용. 주어, 목적어, 보충어 등에서 사용
형용사	명사앞	whose	사람을 나타내며 'whose 명사'형식으로 명사 앞에서 사용.
		what	사물을 나타내며 'what 명사'형식으로 명사 앞에서 사용.
		which	사람, 사물을 나타내며 'which 명사' 형식으로 명사 앞에서 사용.
	보충어	how 어떠한	주어보충어나 목적어 보충어 자리에 '어떠한'의 의미로 사용.
부 사	when 언제		때를 나타낸다.
	where 어디에서		장소를 나타낸다.
	how	어떻게	방법을 나타낸다.
		얼마나	정도를 나타낸다. How old/tall/large/much(명사)/many(명사) etc.
	why 왜		이유를 나타낸다.

⊙ what과 which는 대명사뿐만 아니라 형용사로도 사용된다.

⊙ how는 형용사로서 상태를 나타내어 '어떠한'의 뜻으로 사용된다. 또 부사로 방법을 나타내는 '어떻게'와 정도를 나타내어 '얼마나 ~'로 사용될 수 있다.

A. 의문대명사

who – 누가	whom – 누구를	what – 무엇	which – 어떤 것

① Who – 누가

(a) 주어

- (　　　) is your dad?
  - → Who is your dad?　　　　　　　　　　　누가 너의 아빠야?
- (　　　) would like to go there?
  - → Who would like to go there?　　　　　누가 거기에 가고 싶어?
- (　　　) wants to have a cup of coffee?
  - → Who wants to have a cup of coffee?　　누가 커피를 마시고 싶니?
- (　　　) will be in charge of sales department?
  - → Who will be in charge of sales department?　　누가 판매부 담당이야?

(b) 주어보충어

- This is (　　　)
  - → Who is this?　　　　　　　　　　　　이 사람이 누구야?
- That is (　　　)
  - → Who is that?　　　　　　　　　　　　저 사람이 누구야?

② Whom – 누구를

목적어–목적어자리에서는 whom을 사용하는 것이 원칙이지만 요즈음은 who를 더 많이 사용한다.

- He wants (　　　)
  - → Who(=Whom) does he want?　　　　그는 누구를 원하냐?
- You met (　　　)
  - → Who(=Whom) did you meet?　　　　너는 누구를 만났냐?
- Your sister will marry (　　　)
  - → Who(=Whom) will your sister marry?　너의 누이는 누구와 결혼 할 거야?
- Your brother resembles (　　　)
  - → Who(=Whom) does your brother resemble?　너의 형제는 누구를 닮았어?
- You teach (　　　)
  - → Who(=Whom) do you teach?　　　　너는 누구를 가르치냐?
- The man married (　　　)
  - → Who(=Whom) did the man marry?　그 남자는 누구와 결혼했냐?

③ What – 무엇

(a) 주어
- (　　　) happened?
  → <u>What</u> happened?　　　　　　　　　　　　무슨 일이냐?
- (　　　) made you angry?
  → <u>What</u> made you angry?　　　　　　　　　무엇이 너를 화나게 했냐?

(b) 목적어
- You want (　　　)
  → <u>What</u> do you want?　　　　　　　　　　너는 무엇을 원하냐?
- The teacher teaches (　　　)
  → <u>What</u> does the teacher teach?　　　　그 선생님은 무엇을 가르치니?

(c) 보충어
- That is (　　　)
  → <u>What</u> is that?　　　　　　　　　　　　저것이 무엇이냐?

④ Which – 어떤 것(선택의 대상이 있을 때 사용))

(a) 주어
- (　　　) is higher, this building or that building?
  → <u>Which</u> is higher, this building or that building?　이 빌딩과 저 빌딩 중 어떤 것이 더 높은가요?

(b) 목적어
- You want (　　　), a novel or an essay?
  → <u>Which</u> do you want, a novel or an essay?　소설과 에세이 중 무엇을 원하냐?

(c) 보충어
- What you want is (　　　), love or money.
  → <u>Which</u> is what you want, love or money?　사랑과 돈 중에서 네가 원하는 것은 무엇이냐?

B. 의문형용사

명사 앞			보충어
whose – 누구의	what – 무슨	which – 어떤	how – 어떠한(상태)

1. 명사앞에서 사용하는 의문형용사

① whose
- This is (_____) book.
  - → Whose book is this?　　　　　　　이것이 누구의 책이냐?
- That is (_____) car?
  - → Whose car is that?　　　　　　　저것은 누구의 차냐?

② what
- You like (_____) kind of sports.
  - → What kind of sports do you like?　　너는 어떠한 종류의 스포츠를 좋아하느냐?
- Your boyfriend likes (_____) kind of music.
  - → What kind of music does your boyfriend like?　너의 남자 친구는 어떠한 종류의 음악을 좋아하느냐?

③ which
- You like (_____) movie, a comic or an action?
  - → Which movie do you like, a comic or an action?　너는 어떠한 종류의 스포츠를 좋아하느냐?

2. 보충어에서 사용하는 의문형용사

① how – 어떠한
(a) 주어보충어
- The concert was (_____).
  - → How was the concert?　　　　　　콘서트가 어땠어요?
- Everything is (_____).
  - → How is everything?　　　　　　　잘지내세요?

(b) 목적어보충어
- You like your steak (_____).
  - → How do you like your steak?　　　스테이크를 어떻게 해드릴까요?

C. 의문부사

when – 언제	where – 어디에서	how – 어떻게	why – 왜	how – 얼마나~한

① when – 언제
- You married your wife (   ).
  - → When did you marry your wife?   너의 아내와 언제 결혼했나요?

② where-어디에
- They have a meeting (   ).
  - → Where do they have a meeting?   그들은 어디에서 결혼 했나요?

③ how- 어떻게
- He went to the palace (   ).
  - → How did he go to the palace?   그는 궁궐에 어떻게 갔나요?

④ why-왜
- He went to bed early (   ).
  - → Why did he go to bed early?   그는 왜 일찍 잠자러 갔나요?

⑤ how ~ 얼마나
- Your sister is (   ) old.
  - → How old is your sister?   너의 누이는 몇 살이세요?
- His teacher is (   ) tall.
  - → How tall is his teacher?   너의 선생님의 키는 얼마인가요?
- You have (   ) much money.
  - → How much money do you have?   너는 얼마나 많은 돈을 가지고 있나요?
- Your father has (   ) many books.
  - → How many books does your father have?   너의 아버지는 얼마나 많은 책을 가지고 있나요?

다음 각 괄호안에 들어갈 알맞는 말을 쓰시오.

(01). A: (무엇) do you do when you're stressed out?

B: I usually go for a drive in the country.

(02). A: I haven't seen you for two days. (어디에) have you been?

B: I went to the shopping center, the passport office, and the bank.

(03). A: (왜) did you go to those places?

B: I bought some new clothes at the shopping center, I got my passport at the passport office, and I ordered some traveler's checks at the bank.

(04). A: (어떠한) do you like your new job?

B: I like it very much. The work there is very challenging.

(05). A: (무엇) can I do for you?

B: I'd like to cash this check.

(06). A: (어떠한) do you feel today?

B: I'm feeling much better.

(07). A: (어떤) fruit do you want, bananas or apples?

B: I want apples.

(08). A: (무슨) season do you like?

B: I like spring.

(09). A: (What, Who) animals did you see at the zoo?

B: I saw a lion.

(10). A; (Who, whose) bag was more difficult to lift?

B: Yours

(11). A: Well, he broke his leg.

B: You look pale. (무엇) is wrong?

A: I have a terrible headache.

(12). A: (몇 시) shall we make it?

B: How about 5?

(13). A: (어떠한) would you like your steak?

B: Well-done, please.

(14). A: (얼마나 오래) have you been waiting?

B: For twenty minutes.

(15). A: (무엇) made you think so?

B: Maybe my expectations were too high. I heard so much about it before actually seeing it.

(16). A: (무엇) do you think is the best movie of this year?

B: I think 'Harry Potter and the Order of the Pheonix' is the best. Have you seen it?

(17). A: Hi, long time no see! (어디) have you been?

B: I've been to Australia.

(18). A: Hi. (어디) are you headed?

B: To the library. I'm in a hurry. It will close in 20 minutes.

(19). A: (무엇) are you doing here?

B: I'm waiting for Cindy. She said she'd meet me here at six.

(20). A: (언제) does the library open?

B: It opens at 9 in the morning and closes at 6 in the evening.

(21). A: (언제) are you expecting the baby?

B: Next month. I'm very nervous.

〈정답과 해설 16P〉

Grammar in Reading

〈정답과 해설 17P〉

1. 아래 글을 읽고 답하시오.

W: Good afternoon. ⓐ_____.
M: Yes, please. I'm looking for a T-shirt.
W: How about this one? It's a new style.
M: It looks nice, but I don't like this color. ⓑ You will show me another T-shirt.
W: No problem.

01. ⓐ에 알맞은 말을 쓰시오.

02. ⓑ를 의문문으로 고치시오.

2. 아래 글을 읽고 물음에 답하시오.

Billy : Which club did you joined?
Susan: I joined the Cooking Club. I like cooking. Which club did you join?
Billy : I joined the Book Club.
Susan: (   ) do you usually do in the club?
Billy : We read books and talk about them.

01. 위 글에서 어법상 맞지 않는 것을 찾아 쓰시오.

02. 위 글의 (   ) 안에 들어갈 말을 쓰시오.

3. 아래 글의 (   ) 안에 들어갈 말을 쓰시오.

A: Excuse me, (   ) do I get to the art museum?
B: The art museum? Go up Third Street for two blocks and turn left on Pine Road. Go to the end of the block. The museum is on your left, on the corner of Second Street and Pine Road.
A: Thanks a lot.

Grammar in Reading

〈정답과 해설 17P〉

4. 아래 글의 (   ) 안에 들어갈 말을 쓰시오.

A: You're in good shape. Do you play a lot of sports?

B: Yes, I do. I love sports. I play volleyball on Thursdays, and I play tennis on Saturdays and Sundays.

A: (   ) do you like better?

B: Tennis. It's my favorite.

5. 아래 글의 (   ) 안에 들어갈 말을 쓰시오.

A: Good morning. ⓐ(   ) can I do for you?

B: I bought this book a few days ago,

but there's something wrong with it.

A: ⓑ(무엇) seems to be the problem?

B: Pages 31 to 36 are missing.

Can I exchange this?

01. ⓐ-

02. ⓑ-

6. 아래 글의 (   ) 안에 들어갈 말을 쓰시오.

A: Excuse me, (   ) do you have swimming classes?

B: We have Friday and Saturday classes.

A: How much is it a month?

B: 50,000 won a month.

You can also use the swimming pool every day.

〈정답과 해설 18P〉

1. 다음 문장의 부정문을 각각 쓰시오.

01. You can name the colors.
부정문:

02. You are doing homework.
부정문:

03. The yellow duck is waddling.
부정문:

04. The green frog is about to jump.
부정문:

05. The purple cat is cleaning its front leg.
부정문:

06. The black sheep's fleece was black.
부정문:

07. You may find the blue horse.
부정문:

08. The brown bear was in the forest.
부정문:

09. You see the lion in the zoo.
부정문:

10. She saw a lion and a tiger.
부정문:

11. The animal is white and black.
부정문:

12. The kids want to change the goldfish into a rainbow fish.
부정문:

〈정답과 해설 18P〉

13. Your parents live in Korea.
   부정문:

14. The actress died in 2008.
   부정문:

15. The soldier wants to live.
   부정문:

16. You will see the ghost.
   부정문:

17. You can hear the ghost's cry.
   부정문:

18. The fox caught Rosie.
   부정문:

19. You heard the sound the bees made.
   부정문:

20. The gorilla unlocks the door of his cage.
   부정문:

2. 다음 문장을 각각 부정문과 의문문으로 고치시오.

01. The baby may find the balloon in the picture.
   부정문:
   의문문:

02. Animals wear clothes, too
   부정문:
   의문문:

〈정답과 해설 18P〉

03. Little Bear wants to play outside with clothes on.
   부정문:
   의문문:

04. Little Bear is wearing fur coat.
   부정문:
   의문문:

05. Little Bear made Father Bear with snow.
   부정문:
   의문문:

06. You miss Daddy.
   부정문:
   의문문:

07. You like strawberries like the little Mouse.
   부정문:
   의문문:

08. You can tell me what will happen next.
   부정문:
   의문문:

09. You can open the fingers like Mommy.
   부정문:
   의문문:

10. The professor wrote a book on chemistry.
   부정문:
   의문문:

11. The grocer sells good vegetables and fish.
   부정문:
   의문문:

〈정답과 해설 18~19P〉

12. The architect builds apartment complex.
    부정문:
    의문문:

13. The driver has driven a taxi for 11 years.
    부정문:
    의문문:

14. Ants crawl on the floor.
    부정문:
    의문문:

15. A carpenter put tools on the ground.
    부정문:
    의문문:

16. A carpenter cut steel and wood.
    부정문:
    의문문:

17. The company let us use its parking lot.
    부정문:
    의문문:

18. The player hit the ball over the fence.
    부정문:
    의문문:

19. The bomb burst in the night club.
    부정문:
    의문문:

20. The house cost him a great deal of money.
    부정문:
    의문문:

〈정답과 해설 19P〉

3. 다음 문장의 한글부분을 적절한 의문사를 활용하여 의문문으로 바꾸시오.

01. Bears live 어디.

→

02. 누구 liked red ripe strawberries.

→

03. Mother Bear made 무엇.

→

04. 누구 ate the banana.

→

05. You are 누구.

→

06. Mom is doing 무엇.

→

07. You like 무슨 animal best.

→

08. His brother likes 무슨 subject best.

→

09. You liked 무슨 과목 best.

→

10. You saw 무엇.

→

11. You married 언제.

→

12. Your teacher lives 어디.

→

〈정답과 해설 19P〉

13. The chickens should do 무엇.

  →

14. 무엇 will happen next.

  →

15. Rosie lived 어디.

  →

16. 무엇 is wrong.

  →

17. Your dad was angry 왜.

  →

18. They played 무엇.

  →

19. They look like 무엇.

  →

20. The brown bear is 어디.

  →

4. 다음 문장의 한글부분을 적절한 의문사를 활용하여 의문문으로 바꾸시오.

01. Spot is waving to 누구.

  →

02. There are 얼마나 많은 pigeons.

  →

03. 무엇 came out of the cocoon.

  →

〈정답과 해설 19P〉

04. We wear 무엇.

　→

05. Little Bear will wear 무엇.

　→

06. 누가 is behind the flap.

　→

07. Spot should do 무엇.

　→

08. 누가 is in the middle.

　→

09. The ball is going 어디.

　→

10. That mouse came from 어디.

　→

11. 무엇 runs across the track.

　→

12. It looks like 누구의 shadow.

　→

13. The children are playing 무엇.

　→

14. Spot can get the ball back 어떻게.

　→

15. The duck is doing 무엇 now.

　→

〈정답과 해설 19P〉

16. You like 무슨 freight car.
    →

17. Spot is going to do 무엇 in the park.
    →

18. Monica did 무엇 with the moon.
    →

19. The friend likes 어떤 것, a movie or a music.
    →

20. The fox is following the chicken 왜.
    →

5. 다음 문장의 한글부분을 적절한 의문사를 활용하여 의문문으로 바꾸시오.

01. We can use 얼마나 many different colors.
    →

02. 누구 will get the milk for the bakers.
    →

03. The bakers need 무엇 to bake a cake now.
    →

04. The caterpillar was 무엇 before.
    →

05. The caterpillar ate 무슨 kinds of food.
    →

06. The caterpillar got a stomachache 왜.
    →

〈정답과 해설 19~20P〉

07. Papa took 무엇 along to get the moon.

→

08. Mickey can escape from the batter 어떻게.

→

09. 얼마나 많은 monkeys are jumping on the bed.

→

10. The caterpillar did 무엇 in the cocoon for two weeks.

→

11. The name of the black car was 무엇.

→

12. The freight train went through 어디.

→

13. You like to do 무엇 most in the park.

→

14. You play 어떻게 with the pigeons.

→

15. You want to carry 무엇 in our freight train.

→

16. We can see 무엇 in the sky at night.

→

17. We can see the moon and stars in the sky 언제.

→

18. We can see 무엇 in the sky in the day.

→

〈정답과 해설 20P〉

19. You can see 무엇 in this picture.
→

20. You saw 무슨 kinds of animals in the zoo.
→

6. 다음 문장을 의문문으로 고치시오.

01. You can name the colors.
의문문:

02. You are doing homework.
의문문:

03. The yellow duck is waddling.
의문문:

04. The green frog is about to jump.
의문문:

05. The purple cat is cleaning its front leg.
의문문:

06. The black sheep's fleece is black.
의문문:

07. You can find the blue horse.
의문문:

08. The brown bear is in the forest.
의문문:

09. You saw the lion in the zoo.
의문문:

10. She saw a lion and a tiger.
    의문문:

11. The animal is white and black.
    의문문:

12. The kids want to change the goldfish into a rainbow fish.
    의문문:

13. Your parents live in Korea.
    의문문:

14. The actress died in 2008.
    의문문:

15. The soldier wants to live.
    의문문:

16. You can see the ghost.
    의문문:

17. You can hear the ghost's cry.
    의문문:

18. The fox caught Rosie.
    의문문:

19. You heard the sound the bees made.
    의문문:

20. The gorilla unlocks the door of his cage.
    의문문:

〈정답과 해설 20P〉

7. 다음 문장에서 의문사에 해당되는 부분에 적절한 의문사를 넣어 의문문으로 고치시오.

01. He goes to the library 어떻게.
　　의문문 :

02. He goes 어디 by train.
　　의문문 :

03. Your friend goes to HackWon 언제.
　　의문문 :

04. Your brother goes to Europe 왜.
　　의문문 :

05. He will arrive 언제.
　　의문문 :

06. Your grandfather's birthday is 언제.
　　의문문 :

07. The girl called me 왜.
　　의문문 :

08. You feel 어떠한 today.
　　의문문 :

09. You are going to travel this vacation 어디에.
　　의문문 :

10. Your son doesn't like the teacher 왜.
　　의문문 :

11. Baker finished his homework 언제.
　　의문문 :

12. The weather is 어떠한 in Baekryeong-Do today.
　　의문문 :

〈정답과 해설 20P〉

13. He ate lunch 어디.
   의문문:

14. Your clothes are torn 왜.
   의문문:

15. You go to an English institute 얼마나 자주.
   의문문:

16. The smart phone is 얼마.
   의문문:

17. Your wife is 몇 살.
   의문문:

18. It is from here to SockCho 얼마나 먼.
   의문문:

19. Korea has 얼마나 많은(몇) warships.
   의문문:

20. You have 얼마나 많은(몇) cups of coffee a day.
   의문문:

8. 다음 중 어법상 맞지 않는 것을 찾아 문장을 올바로 쓰시오.

01. Does it looks great?
   (   )

02. Did you finished cooking?
   (   )

03. Do they feel uncomfortable?
   (   )

〈정답과 해설 20P〉

04. Do you need any help with the project?
  (   )

05. Do you wanted me to do it for you?
  (   )

06. Did you wanted me to tell my friends about it?
  (   )

07. Does Alice works for a publishing company?
  (   )

08. Can I picked it up from you now?
  (   )

09. Could you made full payment by Wednesday?
  (   )

10. Are you go to attend the workshop this Saturday?
  (   )

11. Can he gives them out to the people at the workshop?
  (   )

12. Does the office building closes around 7 p.m. Today?
  (   )

13. Does Alice needs to work in the office until late.
  (   )

14. Did you booked a bungalow for our family vacation next month?
  (   )

〈정답과 해설 20P〉

9. 다음 문장에서 잘못된 문장을 찾아 잘못된 부분을 찾아 바르게 고쳐 쓰시오.

01 What does she buys at the market?

(   )

02 How much will you stay in London?

(   )

03 Where does he live with in Seoul?

(   )

04 A: How big is your son? B: He is 5 years old.

(   )

05 A: How many do you go to soccer practice? B: Once a week.

(   )

06. What do you did?

(   )

07. Why it is so important?

(   )

08. Did I left it on again?

(   )

09. What did you thought you should do?

(   )

10. What cause global warming?

(   )

11. What good ideas have you to save energy?

(   )

12. What does you thinks about air pollution?

(   )

〈정답과 해설 21P〉

13. Do you recognizes this island?
    (   )

14. What did Bomi forgot to do?
    (   )

15. May I called attention to this picture?
    (   )

16. Can you saw the difference?
    (   )

17. How did they survived the pressure?
    (   )

18. How animals can see without any light?
    (   )

19. Why the map of Greenland is changing rapidly?
    (   )

20. What has made it possible to explore the deep sea?
    (   )

10. 다음문장에서 어법상 틀린 문장을 찾아 문장을 올바로 다시 고쳐 쓰시오.

01. What I can do for you?
    (   )

02. What do you mean?
    (   )

03. What the prices are?
    (   )

04. When will we leave?
(   )

05. What time is the wedding?
(   )

06. How I may help you?
(   )

07. Where did you bought it?
(   )

08. Which one do he like?
(   )

09. Who want to marry you?
(   )

10. How did Lee Gunhee made much money?
(   )

11. 다음 문장의 밑줄 친 부분을 모른다고 할 때 묻는 의문문을 쓰시오.

01. She is <u>Jane Stone</u>.
→ _____

02. Jane studies <u>English</u>.
→ _____

03. She goes jogging <u>in the morning</u>.
→ _____

04. The actor lives <u>in Seoul</u> now.
→ _____

〈정답과 해설 21P〉

05. You are from <u>Canada</u>?

   → _____

06. You were absent yesterday <u>because I was ill</u>?

   → _____

07. You want <u>a hamburger and cola</u> for lunch?

   → _____

08. He eats <u>bananas and apples</u> for dinner.

   → _____

09. Your mother and you go swimming <u>on Sundays</u>.

   → _____

10. You are crying <u>because of being lonely</u>.

   → _____

memo.

Chapter

06

Exclamatory & Imperative sentences
감탄문과 명령문

Study 01 감탄문(Exclamatory sentence)

놀람 등 감정을 표현하는 문장이다.

명사가 없는 경우		명사가 있는 경우
How 형용사/부사 (주어 +동사)!	단수	What a 형용사 + 단수명사 + (주어 + 동사)!
	복수	What 형용사 + 복수명사 + (주어 + 동사)!

1. 명사가 없는 경우

How 형용사/부사 + 주어 + 동사!

⊙ very나 really 대신에 How를 쓰고 '주어+동사'를 뒤로 뺀다. 끝에 !(감탄사)를 쓴다.

- He is very smart.
  - → How smart he is!　　　　　　　그는 정말 스마트해!
- It is very wonderful.
  - → How wonderful it is!　　　　　　그것 정말 대단해!
- The man is really handsome.
  - → How handsome the man is!　　　그 남자 정말 잘생겼네
- The golden bell flower is very beautiful.
  - → How beautiful the golden bell flower is!　골든 벨 꽃 정말 아름다워!

2. 명사가 있는 경우

What a(n) 형용사 + 단수명사 + (주어 + 동사)!
OR What 형용사 + 복수명사 + (주어 + 동사)!

---

*very나 really 대신에 what을 써서 관사 a(n) 앞에 쓴다. 다음에 '형용사+명사'를 쓰고 '주어+동사'를 뒤에 붙인다.
끝에!(감탄사)를 쓴다. 다만 명사가 복수형일 때는 관사 a(n)을 쓰지 않는다.

- It is a very large stadium.
  → What a large stadium it is!　　　그것 정말 멋진 경기장이네!
- She is a very kind girl.
  → What a kind girl she is!　　　그녀 정말 친절한 소녀네!
- They are very kind girls.
  → What kind girls they are!　　　그들은 정말 친절한 소녀들이야!
- They are really passionate citizens.
  → What passionate citizens they are!　　　그들은 정말 열정적인 시민들이네!

확인문제 1

다음 문장의 빈칸에 how나 what을 넣어 감탄문을 완성하시오.

(01) _____ a nice museum it is!

(02) _____ a high mountain it is!

(03) _____ cute those cats are!

(04) _____ a nice present it is!

(05) _____ funny the movie is!

(06) _____ handsome he is!

(07) _____ pretty she is!

(08) _____ beautiful this garden is!

(09) _____ amazing stories they are!

(10) _____ kind you are!

(11) _____ beautiful buildings they are!

(12) _____ delicious the cheesecake is!

(13) _____ a big dog it is!

(14) _____ a tall man he is!

〈정답과 해설 21P〉

further study

명사주어 be동사 very 형용사.
⇒ 대명사주어 be동사 a(n) very 명사.

{명사주어 be동사 very 형용사.}문장은 {대명사주어 be동사 a(n) very 명사.}로 바꿀 수 있다.

- The boy is very nice. ⇒ He is a very nice boy. 그 소년은 매우 멋져.
- The building is very high. ⇒ It is a very high building. 그 건물은 매우 높아.

◎ 다만 관사 a(n)은 명사가 단수일 때 붙으며 복수일 때는 붙지 않는다.

- The children are very kind. ⇒ They are very kind children. 그 아이들은 매우 친절해.

◎ How 형용사/부사 주어 동사~ & What a 형용사 명사 주어 동사~

이들 문장들은 {명사주어 be동사 very 형용사.}는 {How 형용사/부사 주어 동사!}형태의 감탄문을 만들 수 있다.
또 {대명사주어 be동사 a(n) very 명사.}는 {What [a(n)] 형용사 명사!}형태의 감탄문을 만들 수 있다.

◎ 따라서 위의 문장들은 각각 다음과 같이 감탄문으로 바꿀 수 있다.

- The boy is very nice.→ How nice the boy is! 그 소년은 얼마나 멋진가!
- He is a very nice boy.→ What a nice boy he is! 그는 얼마나 멋진 소년인가?

- The building is very high.→ How high the building is. 그 빌딩은 얼마나 높다는 말인가!
- It is a very high building.→ What a high building it is! 그것은 얼마나 높은 빌딩인가!

- The children are very kind.→ How kind the children are! 그 아이들은 얼마나 친절한가!
- They are very kind children.→ What kind children they are! 그들은 얼마나 친절한 아이들인가!

 확인문제 2

다음 문장을 대명사주어로 사용하여 문장을 각각 전환해 보세요.

01. The mountain is very wonderful.

02. The boys are very smart.

03. The woman is very kind.

04. The cars are very fast.

〈정답과 해설 21P〉

Study 02 명령문(Imperative sentence)

'～해라'–긍정명령문과 '～하지 마라'–부정 명령문이 있다.

긍정 명령문	부정 명령문
앞에 You를 생략하고 동사원형으로 시작한다. 동사가 be동사인 경우는 Be로 시작한다. 강조를 위하여 Do를 쓸 수 있다.	긍정명령문에 앞에 Don't로 넣는다. 강한 부정을 나타내기 위하여 Don't대신 Never를 쓰기도 한다.

1. 긍정명령문

⊙ 동사원형으로 시작된다. 강조를 위해 동사원형 앞에 Do를 쓰기도 한다.

- Speak more slowly.   천천히 말하세요.
- Get out of here.   여기에서 꺼져.
- Calm down.   (강조) Do calm down.   진정해.
- Be careful.   (강조) Do be careful.   조심해
- Be merry.   (강조) Do be merry.   즐겁게 지내.
- Be happy.   (강조) Do be happy.   행복하세요.

2. 부정명령문

⊙ 동사원형 앞에 Don't, Never를 넣는다.

- Don't look at me.   나를 보지 마.
- Don't be gloomy.   우울해 하지 마.
- Never interfere with our work.   결코 우리 일에 간섭하지 마.
- Never do that now.   결코 지금 그것을 하지마세요.

확인문제 3

다음 중 어법상 어색한 부분을 찾아 바르게 고쳐 쓰시오.

(01) Opens it right now!

_____ → _____

(02) Do happy.

_____ → _____

(03) Be not afraid.

_____ → _____

(04) Do kind to the others.

_____ → _____

(05). Doesn't laugh at her!

_____ → _____

(06) Let's swim not here . It's dangerous

_____ → _____

〈정답과 해설 21P〉

further study

'Let's 동사원형~'

'Let's 동사원형~'의 형태의 '~합시다' 표현

	권유, 제안		대답	
하자	Let's + 동사원형 Why don`t we~?	그래, 하자.	Yes, let's. / All right.	
하지말자	Let's not + 동사원형.	아니, 하지말자.	No, let's not.	

⊙'Let's 동사원형~'은 'Shall we 동사원형~?', 'What about 동사원형ing ~?', 'How about 동사원형ing ~?',
' Why don't we 동사원형~?'도 같은 표현이다.

- Let's take a rest. = Shall we take a rest.　휴식을 합시다.
  =What[=How] about taking a rest?　= Why don't we take a rest?
- Let's go to see a movie.　　　　　영화 보러 갑시다.
- Let's fight for democracy.　　　　민주주의를 위해 싸웁시다.

⊙ 다만 '~하지 맙시다'는 'Let's not 동사원형~'의 문장이 된다.

- Let's not drive a car.　　　　　차를 운전하지 맙시다.
- Let's not subscribe to the bad newspaper.　나쁜 신문을 구독하지 맙시다.

 확인문제 4

위에서 배운 내용을 참고하여 다음문장을 완성하시오.

(01) 밖에 나가자.

- Let's go out.
    = Shall _____?
    = What[How] about _____?
    = Why don`t we _____?

(02) 축구를 하자.

- _____ play soccer.
    = Shall we _____?
    = What[How] about _____?
    = Why don't we _____?

(03) 호수에서 수영합시다.

- _____ swim in this lake.
    = Shall we _____ in this lake?
    = What[How] about _____?
    = Why _____?

(04) 화장실을 청소합시다.

- _____ clean the toilet.
    = Shall we _____?
    = How[What] about _____?
    = Why don't we _____?

(05) 독재와 싸웁시다.

- Let's fight against dictatorship.
    = Shall _____ against dictatorship?
    = Why don't _____ against dictatorship?
    = How[What] about _____ against dictatorship?

(06) 잔디밭에서 놀지 맙시다.

- _____ play in the grass.
    =Shall we _____?
    =How[What] about _____?
    = Why don't we _____?

(07) 함께 설거지 합시다.

- _____ wash the dishes together.
    =Shall we _____?
    =How[What] about _____?
    = Why don't we _____?

(08) 민주주의를 위하여 촛불을 켭시다.

- _____ light a candle for democracy.
    = Shall we _____?
    = How[What] about _____?
    = Why don't we _____?

〈정답과 해설 21P〉

Plus UP

'Let me 동사원형~'은 '(당신이) 제가 ~하도록 허락해주세요'라는 뜻으로,
즉 '제가 ~하겠습니다'라는 의미를 나타낸다.

- Let me follow you.　　　　　　　　너를 따르겠어요.
- Let me carry your bag.　　　　　　너의 가방을 들어줄게요.

 확인문제 5

위에서 배운 내용을 참고하여 다음문장을 완성하시오.

(01) 내가 당신을 도와 드리겠습니다.
　　　·Let ＿＿＿＿＿ help you.

(02) 내가 창문을 열겠습니다.
　　　·＿＿＿＿＿ open the window.

(03) 저를 소개하겠습니다.
　　　·＿＿＿＿＿ introduce myself to you.

(04) 내가 사고에 관해서 당신에게 말씀 드리겠습니다.
　　　·＿＿＿＿＿ tell you about the accident.

〈정답과 해설 22P〉

Grammar in Reading

〈정답과 해설 22P〉

1. 아래를 읽고 어법상 틀린 것을 찾아 올바로 고치시오. (틀리지 않은 것도 있음).

To be healthy, it is necessary that you eat nutritious food that your body ⓐ (need) to grow and to be physically active. You may ⓑ (thinks) that you need to make a lot of effort to be healthy. However, this is not true. ⓒ (Starts) with something small that you can do easily. You'll soon ⓓ (realize) that you are healthier. Here ⓔ (is) some tips.

<1>. Eat a healthy, low-fat breakfast such as milk, fruit, rice and soup. Don't ⓕ (skip) breakfast. Eat regular meals.

<2>. Don't eat fast food too often. When you eat fast food, ⓖ (wipes) off the fat before you take a first bite. Don't order large sizes.

<3>. Eat a lot of vegetables and fruit

<4>. Eat healthy snacks.

<5>. Don't ⓗ (used) a remote control when we watch TV.

<6>. Walk to school if you can.

<7>. Take stairs instead of elevators.

<8>. Go out and take a walk. Go swimming and ⓘ (playing) with your friends. Get active!

Let's find some places to rest first.

01. ⓐ –

02. ⓑ –

03. ⓒ –

04. ⓓ –

05. ⓔ –

06. ⓕ –

07. ⓖ –

08. ⓗ –

09. ⓘ –

Grammar in Reading

〈정답과 해설 22P〉

2. 알맞은 단어를 보기에서 찾아 (   ) 안에 넣으시오. 필요시 동사의 형태를 바꾸시오.

raise	repeat	place	hold	get

Today we will learn some yoga moves. You can ⓐ (   ) energy from yoga. It will wake up your muscles. Let's start!

The Tree Pose
Stand up. ⓑ (   ) your right foot and ⓒ (   ) it against your left thigh. Put your hands together. Raise your arms above your head. Try ⓓ (   ) it for 30 seconds. ⓔ (   ) this with your left foot.

01. ⓐ –

02. ⓑ –

03. ⓒ –

04. ⓓ –

05. ⓔ –

⟨정답과 해설 22P⟩

1. 다음 문장을 감탄문으로 고치시오.

01. The game is very exciting.

→

02. The scenery is very wonderful.

→

03. The wind is very tough.

→

04. The cell phone is very cute.

→

05. The Japanese drives a very small car.

→

06. The man has a very nice car.

→

07. Your cousin is a very nice boy.

→

08. Your father has a really expensive car.

→

09. He is very tall.

→

10. It was a very long night

→

11. It is a very great market.

→

12. She is really kind.

→

〈정답과 해설 22~23P〉

2. 다음 문장을 감탄문으로 바꾸시오.

01. It is a very nice movie.
　→What _____ _____ _____ _____ _____!
　→How _____ _____ _____ _____!

02. He is a very kind man.
　→What _____ _____ _____ _____ is!
　→How _____ the man _____!

03. He runs very fast.
　→What _____ _____ runner he _____!
　→How _____ he _____!

04. It was a very long night.
　→ _____!

05. It is a very great market.
　→ _____!

06. She is really kind.
　→ _____!

3. 다음 문장을 감탄문으로 바꾸시오.

01. You are very patient.
　→ _____

02. It is very hot and humid.
　→ _____

03. She is a very smart student.
　→ _____

04. He is a very lazy man.

→ _____

05. They were very angry.

→ _____

06. I was very stupid.

→ _____

07. They were very terrible players.

→ _____

08. She is a very friendly teacher.

→ _____

09. He was very polite.

→ _____

10. These are very beautiful songs.

→ _____

4. 다음 주어진 문장을 감탄문으로 바꾸시오.

01. This car is very expensive.

→ _____

02. You have a very nice car.

→ _____

03. She is a very pretty girl.

→ _____

04. It is very beautiful.

→ _____

05. It is a very high mountain.

→ _____

06. That car is very nice.

→ _____

07. She is very kind.

→ _____

08. He is very handsome.

→ _____

5. 다음 중 어법 상 틀린 문장을 골라 올바로 쓰시오.

01. How beautiful!

02. What a cute girl she is!

03. What old book it is!

04. How wonderful the palaces are!

05. What an interesting party!

06. What a beautiful girl she is!

07. How beautiful is she!

08. What a great poet she is!

09. How a great writer he is!

10. What a wonderful days it is!

〈정답과 해설 23P〉

6. 다음 문장을 괄호 안의 지시대로 바꾸어 쓰시오.

01. You wear a helmet for your own safety. (긍정명령문)
→

02. You are afraid of snakes. (부정명령문)
→

03. You take a bus or a taxi. (긍정명령문)
→

04. You are wrong again. (부정명령문)
→

05. You worry about the test. (부정명령문)
→

06. You are careful. (긍정명령문)
→

07. You are upset. (부정명령문)
→

08. You are ready to go. (긍정명령문)
→

09. You run fast not to be late for class! (긍정명령문)
→

10. You are late for the game. (부정명령문)
→

11. You try this pasta. (긍정명령문)
→

〈정답과 해설 23~24P〉

12. You lie to your friends. (부정명령문)
→

13. You stay up late tonight. (부정명령문)
→

14. You should get up early tomorrow. (긍정명령문)
→

15 You add too much salt. (부정명령문)
→

16. You boil water and cook the noodles. (긍정명령문)
→

17. You mix the noodles with the sauce. (긍정명령문)
→

18. You can add pepper, sesame, and your favorite vegetables. (긍정명령문)
→

19. You cut the onion and garlic into small pieces. (긍정명령문)
→

20. You add the cream sauce and heat it all together. (긍정명령문)
→

7. 다음 문장을 명령문과 부정명령문으로 각각 고치시오.

01. You are late again.
(명령문)   (부정명령문)

02. You are angry to your son.
(명령문)   (부정명령문)

〈정답과 해설 24P〉

03. You are brave to everything.
(명령문)   (부정명령문)

04. You wear a cap.
(명령문)   (부정명령문)

05. You worry about the test.
(명령문)   (부정명령문)

06. You open your book.
(명령문)   (부정명령문)

07. You buy this dictionary.
(명령문)   (부정명령문)

08. You are ready to take a test.
(명령문)   (부정명령문)

09. You turn off the radio.
(명령문)   (부정명령문)

10. You solve the grammar questions.
(명령문)   (부정명령문)

11. You wear a helmet.
(명령문)   (부정명령문)

12. You are afraid of snakes.
(명령문)   (부정명령문)

13. You take a bus or a taxi.
(명령문)   (부정명령문)

14. You eat too much again.
(명령문)   (부정명령문)

〈정답과 해설 24P〉

15. You enter my room.
　　(명령문)　　　　　　　　　　　　　　　　(부정명령문)

16. You are silly.
　　(명령문)　　　　　　　　　　　　　　　　(부정명령문)
　　→

8. 우리말과 일치하도록 괄호 안의 말을 배열하시오.

01. 얼마나 맛있는 치즈 케이크인가!
　　(delicious, how, is, this cheesecake)
　　→

02. 얼마나 그 시험이 어려운지!
　　(difficult, how, is, the test)
　　→

03. 얼마나 지루한 영화인가!
　　(boring, the movie, how, is)
　　→

04. 얼마나 현명한 엄마인가!
　　(wise, mom, how, is)
　　→

05. 그는 얼마나 뛰어난 학생인가!
　　(is, student, what, excellent, an, he)
　　→

〈정답과 해설 24P〉

9. 다음 우리말을 영어로 쓰시오.

01. 정말 아름다운 노래구나!
→

02. 그 소녀 얼마나 키가 큰지!
→

03. 정말 멋진 영화네!
→

04. 정말 멋진 날씨이군!
→

05. 진짜 오래된 컴퓨터구나!
→

06. 정말 좋은 드레스구나!
→

07. 정말 아름다운 꽃들이구나!
→

Chapter

07

Additional questions
부가의문문

부가의문문(동사반대주어의문문) 만드는 법

1. 동사: 앞 문장에서 be/조동사가 있으면, be/조동사를 받는다.

일반동사이면 do/does(3인칭단수)/did(과거)를 쓴다.

2. 반대: 앞에 not등 부정어가 있으면 빼고, 없으면 써준다.

※ not이 있는 경우 반드시 축약형으로 쓴다.

ex) is not → isn't,	are not → aren't
was not → wasn't,	will not → won't
can not → can't	

3. 주어: 주어를 대명사로 써준다.

4. ? 마크한다.

Study 01   be동사나 조동사가 있는 경우

⊙ be/조동사가 있으면 그 be/조동사를 쓰고, not 등 부정어가 없으면 써주고 있으면 안쓴다. 주어를 대명사로 써주고 ?한다.

- He is an architect, isn't he?   그는 건축가이다. 그렇지 않니?
- The players are not careful, are they?   그 선수들 주의 없네, 그렇지요?
- Baker will help the elderly, won't he?   Baker는 노인을 도울 것이다. 그렇지 않니?
- Nelson won't join the game, will he?   Nelson은 그 게임에 참여할 것 같지 않아, 그렇지?
- The turtle can defeat the rabbit in the race, can't it?

거북은 경주에서 토끼를 이길 것이다. 그렇지 않니?

확인문제 1

다음 문장의 빈칸에 알맞은 부가의문문을 써 넣으시오..

(01). It's a good idea, _____ _____ ?

(02). She is pretty, _____ _____ ?

(03). Dad is very busy, _____ _____ ?

(04). His sister isn't a doctor, _____ _____ ?

(05). You are a teacher, _____ _____ ?

(06). The game is exciting, _____ _____ ?

(07). Mom is going to learn English, _____ _____ ?

(08). Your wife wasn't pretty, _____ _____ ?

(09). The women were teachers, _____ _____ ?

(10). The boys were swimming in the river, _____ _____ ?

(11). He can speak Chinese, _____ _____ ?

(12). We can't finish the work, _____ _____ ?

(13). The child couldn't run away, _____ _____ ?

(14). They could swim across the river, _____ _____ ?

(15). The kids can't swim in the sea, _____ _____ ?

(16). They will win the game tomorrow, _____ _____ ?

〈정답과 해설 25P〉

Study 02   일반동사인 경우

⊙ 동사가 be/조동사가 없는 일반동사인 경우, 동사원형이면 do, 동사원형(e)s면 does, 과거동사이면 did를 쓴다. not등 부정어가 없으면 써주고 있으면 안쓴다. 주어를 대명사로 써주고 ?한다.

1. 동사원형인 경우-do/don't ~ ?

- They **play** baseball in the ground, don't they? 그들은 운동장에서 야구를 한다. 그렇지 않니?
- You **buy** too much stationery, don't you? 너는 너무 많은 문구류를 산다. 안 그래?
- The sick **don't want** to see a doctor, do they? 그 아픈 사람들은 진료를 원하지 않는다. 그렇지?

2. 주어가 3인칭 단수이고 현재인 경우, 즉 동사원형(e)s일 때 does/doesn't ~?

- Mr. Kim **wants** to buy a car, doesn't he? 김씨는 차를 사는 것을 원해, 그렇지 않니?
- Miss. Lee **doesn't go** to temple every Sunday, does she?
미스 리가 매주 절에 가는 것은 아니다. 그렇지?

3. 과거형 동사인 경우– did/didn't ~?

• You <u>failed</u> in the exam, did n't you?　　　너는 그 시험에 실패했다. 안 그래?

• Miss. Park <u>didn't steal</u> the book, did she?　　미스 박이 그 책을 훔치지 않았다.

🔍 확인문제 2

다음 문장의 빈칸에 알맞은 부가의문문을 써 넣으시오.

(01). You love him, _____ _____ ?

(02). Ellice didn't go there, _____ _____ ?

(03). You need a bike, _____ _____ ?

(04). My brother needs a pen-pal, _____ _____ ?

(05). She doesn't go to school, _____ _____ ?

(06). Peter sold the doughnuts, _____ _____ ?

(07). My sister doesn't love him, _____ _____ ?

(08). Cindy lay on the mattress, _____ _____ ?

(09). That shirt looks great, _____ _____ ?

(10). Jenny loves to play the violin, _____ _____ ?

(11). Sally speaks English well, _____ _____ ?

(12). My friends played baseball every weekend, _____ _____ ?

〈정답과 해설 25P〉

다만 명령문은 긍정이든 부정이든 'will you?', 'Let's ~'는 'shall we?'를 쓴다.

- Drive a car carefully, will you?
- Don't come into the grass, will you?
- Don't drive a car in this area, will you?
- Let's go to the mountain, shall we?
- Let's sweep off the snow in front of our house, shall we?

차를 조심히 운전하세요, 그렇지요?
잔디밭에 들어가지 마시오, 그렇지요?
이 지역에서 운전하지 마세요, 그렇지요?
산에 갑시다. 그렇지요?

우리 집앞에 눈을 치웁시다. 그렇지요?

확인문제 3

다음 문장의 빈칸에 알맞은 부가의문문을 써 넣으시오.

(01). Clean your room, _____ _____ ?

(02). Wash your hands, _____ _____ ?

(03). Don't close the door, _____ _____?

(04). Let's go to the park, _____ _____?

(05). Let's take a rest, _____ _____?

(06). Let's go for a walk, _____ _____ ?

(07). Don't be late, _____ _____ ?

(08). Let's go fishing, _____ _____ ?

〈정답과 해설 25P〉

Plus UP | have/has, had

A. 일반동사

- They have much money, don't they?

  그들은 많은 돈을 가지고 있다. 그렇지 않니?

- You had a big house, didn't you?

  너는 큰 집을 가지고 있었다. 그렇지 않니?

B. 조동사적 성격

- The woman has studied English for 15 years old, hasn't she?

  그 여자는 15년 동안 영어를 공부해왔다. 그렇지 않니?

- The woman had already finished reading the book, hadn't she?

  그 여자는 이미 그 책을 읽는 것을 끝마쳤다. 그렇지 않냐?

확인문제 4

다음 문장의 빈칸에 알맞은 부가의문문을 써 넣으시오.

(01). She has been to England, _____ _____?

(02). Peter has taken a walk, _____ _____?

(03). They have many books, _____ _____?

(04). Paul has never been to the museum, _____ _____ ?

(05). The young man has a big house, _____ _____?

(06). We have met the president two times, _____ _____?

〈정답과 해설 25P〉

Grammar in Reading

〈정답과 해설 25P〉

1. 다음 문장을 읽고 (   ) 안에 알맞은 부가의문문을 쓰시오.

Hi! I often think about you. What do you do?
You have a child, ⓐ (   )? Is taking pictures still your favorite

hobby? What do you look like? You don't have pimples, ⓑ (   )?
Please say "no." They are bothering me now. Anyway, I bet you are cool now, right? Haha!

01. ⓐ-   02. ⓑ-

2. 다음 문장을 읽고 (   ) 안에 알맞은 부가의문문을 쓰시오.

Finally, I am going to make a promise to you. I often get up late and have to hurry in the morning.
That's not a good habit, (   )? So I am going to try to become an early bird. Also, I am going
to keep a diary every day. These are good promises, (   )? Anyway, I hope you like my
promises.
Love,
Fifteen-year-old Siwon

01. ⓐ-   02. ⓑ-

Grammar in Reading

〈정답과 해설 25~26P〉

3. 다음 글을 읽고 물음에 답하시오.

In English-speaking countries, people say "cheese" when they take a picture. How about in Korea? You know the answer, ⓐ (   )? Many people say "gimchi," of course. When people say "cheese" or "gimchi," they smile. What else do these foods have in common? Surprisingly, both are full of bacteria. You cannot see bacteria, ⓑ (   )? They are very small. But they live everywhere–in the air, in the ground, in water, and even inside your body. Some bacteria cause diseases. Others grow on food and spoil it. These bacteria are bad, ⓒ (   )?

위 글의 빈칸 ⓐ, ⓑ, ⓒ에 들어갈 부가의문문이 다음 빈칸에 들어갈 말과 각각 같은 것을 고르시오?

① The classroom is too cold, _____?

② You feel freezy, _____?

③ You can't finish your work, _____?

④ All Jeniffer's friends are pretty, _____?

⑤ Sera is playing the guitar, _____?

01. ⓐ-   02. ⓑ-   03. ⓒ-

4. 아래 대화의 빈칸에 알맞은 부가의문문 표현을 쓰시오.

W: How was your business trip to London?

M: You won't believe it, but it was a total disaster.

W: What happened?

M: When I arrived in London, I couldn't find my baggage. It took two days for me to claim it.

W: That happened to me when I went to the USA. It's really frustrating,(   )?

M: It sure is. There's more. I got pickpocketed on the subway on the third day of my trip.

W: No way! That sounds awful.

M: Yeah. I got really mad. But that's not even the end of it.

W: You're kidding.

M: On the day I headed back to Korea, my flight was delayed 12 hours because of bad weather.

W: You really had terrible luck.

정답:_____

중간 · 기말고사 내신만점대비문제

1. 다음 문장의 부가의문문을 쓰시오.

01. Be silent, (   )?

02. She was a fairy writer, (   )?

03. Don't make a noise, (   )?

04. Choose the book, (   )?

05. Close the books, (   )?

06. Let's not make a trouble, (   )?

07. Let's not cut the pine tree, (   )?

08. Let's plant a tree in the garden, (   )?

09. The oxen can swim in the river, (   )?

10. The sick boy can not run fast, (   )?

11. The public toilets in the park are not clean, (   )?

12. They have visited the city sever times, (   )?

2. 다음 문장의 괄호 안에서 알맞은 것을 고르시오.

01. He can't play the flute, (does he, can he)?

02. Your sister will come here, (won't she, will she)?

03. Come home early, (will you, shall we)?

〈정답과 해설 26P〉

04. Let's watch television, (will we, shall we)?

05. You are a student, (aren't you, are you)?

06. Nancy isn't a tennis player, (is Nancy, is she)?

07. There is a horse on the field, (isn't it, isn't there)?

08. She has a science book, (doesn't she, hasn't she)?

09. Your father speaks English very well, (doesn't he, didn't he)?

10. They don't listen to music, (do they, don't they)?

11. Suji didn't clean her room, (did she, didn't she)?

12. You joined our club, (did you, don't you, didn't you)?

3. 다음 문장의 빈칸에 알맞은 부가의문문을 써 넣으시오.

01. Stop running, _____ ?

02. Copy machines can work fast, _____ ?

03. Kelly didn't sleep well last night, _____ ?

04. The bending machine isn't raining, _____ ?

05. You have a pretty pet, _____ ?

06. Calton and I are in the same class, _____ ?

07. The boys won't go to the gym, _____ ?

〈정답과 해설 26P〉

08. You aren't a good marathoner, _____ ?

09. The boys and girls were so noisy, _____ ?

10. These aren't your smart phones, _____ ?

11. Let's take a rest now, _____ ?

12. My mom doesn't know him, _____ ?

13. Mom heats the vegetable oil in a small pan, _____ ?

14. Cook the onion and garlic until they become brown. _____ ?

15. You can enjoy different kinds of spaghetti, _____ ?

16. Call me tonight as soon as you arrive at the station. _____ ?

4. 다음 문장에서 어법상 어색한 부분을 찾아 바르게 고쳐 쓰시오.

01. She likes Keller, did she?
_____ → _____

02. Jim didn't do his homework yet, didn't he?
_____ → _____

03. Mina can't swim in the sea, can't she?
_____ → _____

04. You won't go with us, don't you?
_____ → _____

05. She doesn't like vegetables, do she?
_____ → _____

〈정답과 해설 26P〉

06. Ann is going to have a birthday, doesn't she?

_____ → _____

07. Chagall painted great pictures, didn't Chagall?

_____ → _____

08. Tom and Mary are an astronaut, aren't Tom and Mary ?

_____ → _____

09. The last train left already, did they?

_____ → _____

10. Mike has many books, don't Mike?

_____ → _____

5. 다음 문장에서 부가의문문이 어법상 맞지 않는 것을 찾아 올바로 고치시오.

01. The man has a car, hasn't he?

02. Let's go shopping, aren't we?

03. She never goes out with his pet dog, doesn't she?

04. Amy wrote this story before, didn't she?

05. The boys have finished their homework, don't they?

06. You are reading Peter Pan, are you?

07. Peter Pan can fly, can't he?

08. You like this story, doesn't you?

09. Jennifer is his friend, isn't she?

10. Captain Hook doesn't like Peter Pan, do they?

11. You didn't see him yesterday, do you?

12. My parents were kind to him, weren't they?

13. David isn't going to go on a bike trip, isn't he?

14. The princess could save Snow White, couldn't she?

15. Jane's clothes are as colorful as Yumin's, isn't she?

16. Please sing a song for us, don't you?

17. Don't speak loudly in class, shall you?

18. Let's listen to the teacher, shall we ?

19. He won't buy the desk, won't he?

20. Bill and Jane like fish, don't he?

6. 다음 우리말과 뜻이 같도록 ( ) 안의 어구를 사용하여 문장을 쓰시오.

01. 학교에 늦지 마라, 알았지?
   (school. late)
   → _____

02. 지금 캠핑 가자, 응?
   (go camping)
   → _____

03. 너는 노래를 아주 잘 할 수 있지, 그렇지 않니?
   (sing well)
   → _____

〈정답과 해설 27P〉

04. 그는 화를 내요, 그렇지 않나요?

(angry)

→ _____

05. 당신은 점심을 먹지 않았지요. 그렇죠?

(have lunch)

→ _____

06. 날씨가 춥다, 그렇지 않나요?

(cold)

→ _____

07. 그는 매우 똑똑해, 그렇지 않니?

(very smart)

→ _____

08. 다시는 같은 실수를 반복하지 마라, 알겠니?

(the same, make, mistake)

→ _____

09. Sora는 지금 집에서 쉬고 있는 중이다. 그렇지 않니?

(relax, at home)

→ _____

10. 친구들과 싸우지 마라. 알았지?

(fight, friends, with)

→ _____

11. 너는 거기에서 사람들을 볼 수 있어, 그렇지 않니?

(the people, see)

→ _____

12. 그들은 그 소녀의 가장 좋아하는 가수를 보고 있는 중이다. 그렇지 않니?

(looking at, favorite, the girl's, singer)

→ _____

Chapter

08

Pronoun for person
사람을 나타내는
대명사와 위치

사용되는 자리에 따라 달라지는 사람을 나타내는 사람대명사

인칭	수와 성		주격-주어용 (~은/는/이/가)	소유격 명사 앞에서 명사를 수식하는 형용사역할	목적격-목적어용 (동사와 전치사 의 목적어) (~을/~에게)	소유대명사 (소유격 + 명사) (~의 것)	재귀대명사 다시 돌아온 대명사 (~자신)
1인칭	단수		I	my	me	mine	myself
	복수		we	our	us	ours	ourselves
2인칭	단수		you	your	you	yours	yourself
	복수		you	your	you	yours	yourselves
3인칭	단수	남성	he	his	him	his	himself
		여성	she	her	her	hers	herself
		중성	it	its	it	–	itself
	복수		they	their	them	theirs	themselves

1. 주격

⊙ 주어 자리에 쓰인다. 보통 '~은(는), ~가, ~이' 등으로 해석한다.

- I want to go to the party. 　　　　　　　나는 파티에 가는 것을 원한다.
- We met our friends in the party. 　　　　우리는 파티에서 우리의 친구들을 만났다.
- You are good at speaking English 　　　너는 영어를 말하는데 잘한다.
- He joined the club of nature environment preservation.
　　　　　　　　　　　　　　　　　　그는 자연환경보호클럽에 가입했다.
- She encourages her husband to begin his new work.
　　　　　　　　　　　　　그녀는 그녀의 남편이 그의 새로운 일을 시작하도록 격려한다.

 **확인문제** 1

아래의 빈칸을 각각 채우시오.

주격	소유격	목적격	소유대명사	재귀대명사
I	my	(01).	(02).	myself
we	(03).	us	(04).	(05).
you(단수)	(06).	(07).	yours	(08).
you(복수)	your	you	(09).	(10).
he	(11).	(12).	his	(13).
she	(14).	(15).	(16).	herself
it	(17).	(18).	–	(19).
they	(20).	(21).	(22).	(23).

〈정답과 해설 27P〉

2. 소유격

⊙ 명사 앞에서 '~의'에 해당되고 형용사의 일종으로 볼 수 있다.

• That is my apartment.	저것은 나의 아파트다.
• This is our school.	이것은 우리 학교다.
• I went to your office.	나는 나의 사무실을 갔다.
• That is his father.	저것은 그의 아버지다.
• We played together with her brother.	우리는 그녀의 형과 함께 놀았다.
• Their school stands near the river.	그들의 학교는 강 가까이에 서있다.

3. 목적격

⊙ 목적어가 필요한 동사나 전치사 뒤에 쓰인다. '~을(를)'로 해석한다.

1. 동사의 목적어

- Mom punished me.   엄마는 나를 처벌했다.
- Our teacher praised us.   우리 학교는 우리들을 칭찬했다.
- We will follow you.   우리는 너를 다를 것이다.
- They criticized him.   그들은 그를 비판했다.
- My cousin married her.   나의 삼촌은 그녀와 결혼했다.

2. 전치사의 목적어

- I am with you.   너에게 동의해.
- Sandra lives with him.   Sandra는 그와 함께 산다.
- Eunice works for you.   Eunice는 너를 위해 일해.
- The police run after them.   경찰은 그들을 추적해.
- My friends want to go there with me.   나의 친구들은 우리와 거기를 가기를 원해.
- The children went camping with us.   아이들은 우리와 캠핑갔다.
- The students's parents joined for them. 학생들의 부모는 그들을 위해 합류했다.

4. 소유대명사

⊙ '~의 것'에 해당하는 말로 소유격과 명사가 합해진 것이다.

- That car is mine(=my car).   저 차는 나의 것이다.
- The library is ours(=our library).   그 도서관은 우리들의 것이다.
- The books are yours(=your books).   그 책들은 너의 것이다.
- That bag is his(=his bag).   저책은 그의 것이다.
- The signature is hers(=her signature).   그 서명은 그녀의 것이다.

확인문제 2

다음 문제에서 빈칸을 보기에서 찾아 채우시오.

I	my	me	mine	myself

(01). The amazing wonders await (　　　)

(02). The surprising guests wait for (　　　)

(03). That bag is (　　　)

(04). I train (　　　) to breathe deep.

(05). (　　　) had breakfast at 7.

(06). That is (　　　) car.

〈정답과 해설 27P〉

확인문제 3

다음 문제에서 빈칸을 보기에서 찾아 채우시오.

we	our	us	ours	ourselves

(01). The library is (　　　).

(02). We must help (　　　).

(03). (　　　) love nature.

(04). This is (　　　) school.

(05). The soldiers help (　　　).

〈정답과 해설 27P〉

확인문제 4

다음 문제에서 빈칸을 보기에서 찾아 채우시오.

| you | your | you | yours | yourself / yourselves |

(01). This is (   ) grandmother.

(02). The teacher wants to meet (   ).

(03). Is this smart phone (   )?

(04). You must train (   )

(05). How much rain falls where (   ) live?

(06). Ask a partner to name (   ) plant or animal.

(07). (   ) can achieve your dream.

〈정답과 해설 27P〉

확인문제 5

다음 문제에서 빈칸을 보기에서 찾아 채우시오.

| he | his | him | his | himself |

(01). That house is (   )

(02). The actor trained (그 자신)

(03). (   ) saw an oak tree and a fern.

(04). The police officer arrested (   )

(05). Andrew Seto went for a walk in the woods near (   ) school.

〈정답과 해설 27P〉

확인문제 6

다음 문제에서 빈칸을 보기에서 찾아 채우시오.

she	her	her	hers	herself

(01). Rosa Park loves (그녀 자신)

(02). (　　　) would like to buy a small car.

(03). I asked (　　　) to clean the classroom.

(04). My house is larger than (　　　)

(05). (　　　) car is more expensive than mine

〈정답과 해설 28P〉

확인문제 7

다음 문제에서 빈칸을 보기에서 찾아 채우시오.

it	its	it	itself

(01). Honesty thrives (　　　).

(02). (　　　) leaves can get light.

(03). The plant can hold water in (　　　) thick stem.

(04). (　　　) waxy covering helps keep water in.

(05). The tortoise gets water from (　　　) food.

(06). Where does (　　　) live?

(07). A bear needs a large part of a forest for (　　　) habitat.

(08). Use it to describe (　　　) shape.

(09). History repeats (그것 자신).

〈정답과 해설 28P〉

확인문제 8

다음 문제에서 빈칸을 보기에서 찾아 채우시오.

> they   their   them   theirs   themselves

(01). (   ) need water and light.

(02). (   ) leaves can get the light they need.

(03). Observe (   ) for two hours.

(04). Put (   ) in a sunny place.

(05). The bags are (   ).

(06). Heaven helps those who help (그들 자신들).

(07). Observe the animals. How are (   ) alike?

(08). When you classify animals, you group (   ) by ways they are alike.

(09). Some ocean animals swim to find (   ) food.

〈정답과 해설 28P〉

5. 재귀대명사

⊙ '-self/selves' 형태로 명사나 대명사를 다시 쓴다는 말이다. 명사나 대명사를 강조하는 강조용법과 주어가 동사나 전치사의 목적어에 다시 쓰인 것이 있다.

1. 강조용법 – 생략해도 강조의 의미만 없어질 뿐 문장은 성립한다.

① 주어강조

주어를 강조할 경우, 주어 바로 뒤에 쓰거나 문장 끝에 쓸 수 있다.

- We ourselves became reptiles.
    = We became reptiles ourselves.   우리자신이 파충류가 되었다.
- I myself teach my son German.
    = I teach my son German myself.   나 자신이 나의 아들에게 독일어를 가르친다.

- You yourself must do it .
  - = You must do it yourself.　　　　　　　　　너는 너 자신이 직접 그것을 행해야 한다.
- We ourselves prepare our admission fee for the university.
  - = We prepare our admission fee for the university ourselves.

    　　　　　　　　　　　　　　　　　　　　우리 자신들이 대학 입학금을 직접 준비한다.
- You yourself finished your homework.
  - =You finished your homework yourself.　　너 자신이 너의 숙제를 끝냈다.
- Steve Jobs himself made I-phone.
  - = Steve Jobs made I-phone himself.　　　스티브잡스 자신이 아이폰을 만들었다.
- Rosa Parks herself fought against the unjust law, Jim Crow law.
  - = Rosa Parks fought against the unjust law, Jim Crow law herself.

    　　　　　　　　　　　　　　　로자팍스 그녀자신이 부당한 법, 짐크로우법안에 반대하여 싸웠다.
- The workers themselves fight for their rights.
  - = The workers fight for their rights themselves.

    　　　　　　　　　　　　　　　그 노동자들 자신들이 그들의 권리를 위하여 싸웠다.

② 목적어강조

　목적어에 나온 (대)명사를 강조하는 경우도 있다.
- Mike has seen Mary herself.(Mary=herself)　　마이크가 메리 바로 그녀를 보았다.
- Heidi married the prince himself.(the prince=himself)　하이디는 그 왕자와 결혼했다.

2. 재귀용법 – 주어가 동사나 전치사 다음에 다시 오는 경우. 생략하면 목적어가 없어지므로 문장이 성립하지 않는다.
　　　　　　절대 생략 불가.

① 동사의 목적어
- An ant licks itself.　　　　　　　　　　　개미가 자기 자신을 핥는다.
- The ants clean themselves.　　　　　　　개미들이 스스로를 청결하게 한다.
- I don't like myself.　　　　　　　　　　　나는 자신을 좋아하지 않는다.
- We must love ourselves.　　　　　　　　우리는 우리 자신을 사랑해야 한다.
- John Nar praised himself.　　　　　　　존 나르는 자신을 칭찬했다.
- Alice criticized herself.　　　　　　　　앨리스는 그녀 자신을 비판했다.
- The players train themselves for muscular strength.

　　　　　　　　　　　　　　　　　그 선수들은 근력을 위해 자신들을 훈련한다.

② 전치사의 목적어

for oneself (다른 사람 도움 없이) 혼자 힘으로	by oneself (= alone) 혼자서
of itself(=spontaneously) 저절로	beside oneself 제정신이 아닌

- Draw a picture for yourself.　　　　　　　네 스스로 그림을 그려라.

- The radio turned on of itself.   그 라디오는 저절로 켜졌다.
- You can study math for yourself.   너는 스스로 수학을 공부한다.
- Alice lives by herself.   앨리스는 혼자서 산다.
- The reporters report nowadays **beside** themselves.

         그 기자들은 요즈음 제정신이 아닌 채 보도한다.
- Anna studies English for herself.   안나는 영어를 혼자서 공부한다.
- Jung Yak-Young wrote over 500 books for himself.

         정약용은 혼자서 500권 이상의 책을 썼다.
- Two Koreas must achieve a unification for themselves.

         남북한은 스스로 통일을 이루어야 한다.

 확인문제 9

다음 문장들에서 사용된 -self/-selves가 생략이 가능한 '강조용법'인지 생략할 수 없는 '재귀대명사 용법'인지를 말하시오.

(01). Ivan supported himself.

(02). Defend yourselves now.

(03). She herself made a doll.

(04). He himself was often sick.

(05). We should take care of ourselves.

(06). I myself made this beautiful necklace.

(07). His mother herself killed a mosquito

(08). My cousin himself was often sick.

(09). My daughter bought this for me herself.

(10). Juliet stabbed herself through her heart.

〈정답과 해설 28P〉

명사의 격

명사는 주어자리에 쓰이는 주격, 목적어 자리에 쓰이는 목적격은 명사 그 자체이다.
소유격과 소유대명사는 '명사's'로 같다. 명사의 재귀대명사는 각각 남자 한명은 himself, 여자 한명은 herself, 사물하나는 itself, 사람, 사물의 둘 이상이면 themselves 등 대명사의 재귀대명사를 사용한다.

예를 들어

주어자리	소유격자리	동사, 전치사의 목적어 자리	소유대명사	재귀대명사
Jennifer	Jennifer's	Jennifer	Jennifer's	herself
Michael	Michael's	Michael	Michael's	himself
a student	a student's	a student	a student's	himself / herself
students	students'	students	students'	themselves

Jennifer studies Chinese.   제니퍼는 중국어를 공부한다.

This is Jennifer's book.   이것은 제니퍼의 책이다.

They love Jennifer.   그들은 제니퍼를 사랑한다.

That car is Jennifer's.   저 차는 제니퍼의 것이다.

Jennifer trains herself.   제니퍼는 그녀 자신을 스스로 훈련하다.

Michael enjoys himself.   마이클은 스스로를 즐긴다.

The students investigate the incident for themselves.

학생들 스스로 그 사건을 조사한다.

Grammar in Reading

〈정답과 해설 28P〉

1. 다음 문장의 ( ) 안에 주격, 소유격, 목적격 등 알맞은 형태의 인칭대명사를 쓰시오.

[Cell phone rings.]

M: Mom. I was just about to call ⓐ (너).

W: Malcolm, where are you? We're supposed to have dinner together for Grandma's birthday.

M: I know, but I don't think I can make it.

W: Are ⓑ (너) still doing ⓒ (너) group assignment at school?

M: No. I've already completed the report for the presentation.

W: Then, what's the problem?

M: On ⓓ (나) way home, when I transferred to Line 1, I accidentally left my bag on the shelf of the subway.

W: You mean you lost ⓔ (너) bag on the subway?

M: Yes… and the USB drive was in the bag. ⓕ (나) group's report is in it.

W: Oh, no! What are ⓖ (너) going to do?

M: Well… I'm just heading for the lostandfound now.

W: Don't worry tooch. I'm sure ⓗ (너) will get it back.

01. ⓐ–
02. ⓑ –
03. ⓒ –
04. ⓓ –
05. ⓔ –
06. ⓕ –
07. ⓖ –
08. ⓗ –

Grammar in Reading

〈정답과 해설 28~29P〉

2. 다음 문장의 ( ) 안에 주격, 소유격, 목적격 등 알맞은 형태의 인칭대명사를 쓰시오.

M: Susan, I heard ⓐ (너) were a straight A student last semester. What's ⓑ (너) secret?

W: Well, I believe ⓒ (나) secret is the great saying "Know Yourself."

M: What do you mean?

W: I mean that I know which learning style is best for ⓓ (나).

M: Can you tell ⓔ (나) more about ⓕ (너) learning style?

W: I'm a physical learner. Using my body, hands, and my sense of touch enhances my learning.

M: That's impressive! How did ⓖ (너) discover your learning style?

W: I took a test online. Why don't you give it a try?

M: Sure, I'll try it. Do you think I'll get good grades in school if I use ⓗ (나) own learning style?

W: Of course. I'm sure it'll work for ⓘ (너).

M: Thanks for the advice.

01. ⓐ –   02. ⓑ –   03. ⓒ –
04. ⓓ –   05. ⓔ –   06. ⓕ –
07. ⓖ –   08. ⓗ –   09. ⓘ –

3. 다음 문장의 ( ) 안에 주격, 소유격, 목적격 등 알맞은 형태의 인칭대명사를 쓰시오.

It's a hot summer day. Dave and ⓐ (그) mother are reading books in the living room with the electric fan on. Even with the fan, it's still so hot that ⓑ (그) can't focus on his book. Dave is sweating and asks ⓒ (그) mother to switch on the airconditioner. ⓓ (그녀) agrees that it's time to start using it and allows ⓔ (그) to turn it on. Dave rushes to the airconditioner with a big smile. Suddenly, ⓕ (그녀) remembers reading an article about the dangers of dust in air conditioners. The article said it's important to keep them clean. ⓖ (그녀) really wants to remove the dust from the filter before using it. Dave is about to hit the "ON" button.

01. ⓐ –   02. ⓑ –   03. ⓒ –
04. ⓓ –   05. ⓔ –   06. ⓕ –
07. ⓖ –

Grammar in Reading

〈정답과 해설 29P〉

4. 다음 문장의 ( ) 안에 주격, 소유격, 목적격 등 알맞은 형태의 인칭대명사를 쓰시오.

M: Hi, Sarah. You look so busy.

W: Yeah, I'm a little busy. I'm helping my father with ⓐ (그) new business.

M: Your father started a new business? Wasn't ⓑ (그) an engineer?

W: Right, but ⓒ (그) retired and opened a guesthouse for foreigners.

M: Wow! That sounds fantastic. How are you helping him?

W: I'm trying to make an online advertisement for my father's guesthouse, but it's not that easy.

M: What's the problem?

W: Well, many Chinese travellers are coming to this area, so I'd like to make an advertisement in Chinese, but I'm not good at Chinese.

M: Don't worry. I have a friend, Jason, who is majoring in Chinese.

W: Really? Do you think ⓓ (그) would be willing to help me with some translations?

M: Yes, I'm sure ⓔ (그) can translate ⓕ (너) advertisement into Chinese.

01. ⓐ –　　　　　　　02. ⓑ –　　　　　　　03. ⓒ –
04. ⓓ –　　　　　　　05. ⓔ –　　　　　　　06. ⓕ –

5. 다음 대화를 읽고 요약할 때 ( ) 안에 알맞은 인칭 대명사를 넣으시오.

Brian: Sujin, what are you going to do this weekend?

Sujin: I'm going to visit my grandparents in Daejeon with my brother.

Brian: Wow, just you and your brother? Are you going to go by bus?

Sujin: No, I'm going to take the train.

Brian: Sounds great. Have a nice trip.

Sujin: Thanks.

→　Sujin and ⓐ (그녀) brother are going to visit ⓑ (그들) grandparents in Daejoen this weekend.
　　ⓒ (그들) will get there by train. Brian tells ⓓ (그녀) to have a nice trip.

01. ⓐ –　　　　　　　02. ⓑ –　　　　　　　03. ⓒ –
04. ⓓ –

〈정답과 해설 30P〉

1. (   )안에 알맞은 형태를 고르시오.

01. Ask (you, yourself)

02. Cathy believes (her, herself) beautiful.

03. Jenny will tell (his, him) the truth.

04. Did (they, them) visit you last month?

05. They brought (our, us) some sandwiches.

06. Were (your, you) predictions correct?

07. Communicate with (your, you) partners.

08. Charlie cooked the duck by (him, himself)

09. Heidi wrote the fork song for (her, herself)

10. We gave (them, themselves) something to eat.

11. The widow can't live by (her, herself)

12. The divorced man lived by (him, himself)

13. The fox looked at (it, itself) in the mirror.

14. The players are proud of (them, themselves)

15. The man asked (her/herself) to clean the room.

2. ( )안에 알맞은 형태를 고르시오.

01. Kevin and I enjoyed (us, ourselves) at the game.

02. A girl looked at (her/herself) through the window.

03. We saw (your, yours) mom on the way to school.

04. Charlie introduced (us, ourselves) to the grandfather.

05. Mr Winka lent (her, herself) the dictionary last night.

06. I've eaten Minsu's cake. I didn't know it was (him, his).

07. John and you went to the movies. (You, Your) had fun.

08. Thank you for helping me. (You, Your) are very kind.

09. Do you know the gentleman over there? What is (his, him) name?

10. Did you see the dogs in the picture? Those are (her, hers).

11. Mrs. Han wanted to see my family, so she invited (we, us) to dinner.

12. Susan is my brother's friend. I don't know (she, her) very well.

13. The manager heard the news but he didn't realize (it's, its) importance.

14. After two weeks, each caterpillar transforms (it, itself).

15. The butterflies that flew south do not return north (them, themselves)

〈정답과 해설 30P〉

3. 다음 문장들에서 사용된 –self/–selves가 생략이 가능한 '강조용법'인지 생략할 수 없는 '재귀대명사 용법'인지를 말하시오.

01. My brother painted all the fences himself.

02. She will love only herself, and no others.

03. Please help yourself at my birthday party.

04. Heaven helps those who help themselves.

05. Our new teacher introduced himself to us.

06. The children themselves cleaned the room.

07. The old potter completed the mission himself.

08. Rosaline keeps herself pure for the remainder of her life.

09. The young mechanic transformed himself into a merchant.

10. The skirts and pants were embroidered by Annie herself.

Chapter 09

Pronouns & Nouns

셀 수 있는 명사와 셀 수 없는 명사를 받는 대명사들

Study **01**

many, a few, few & much, a little, little

Study **02**

all, most, a lot/lots, half, some, none

Study **03**

some(thing, body)과 any(thing, body)

셀 수 있는 명사와 셀 수 없는 명사를 받는 수와 양을 표현하는 구체적으로 정하지 않는 대명사들. 단 <u>청색</u>은 **대명사기능**과 **형용사기능**이 있다.

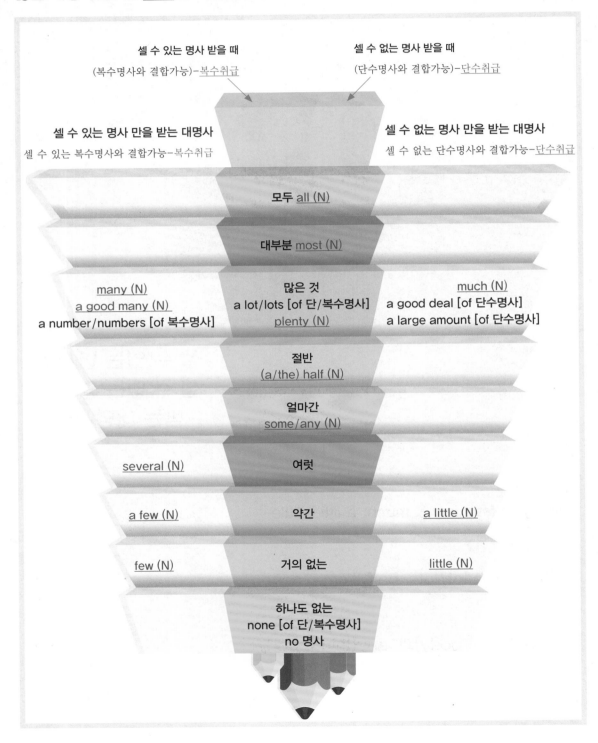

셀 수 있는 명사 받을 때
(복수명사와 결합가능)–<u>복수취급</u>

셀 수 없는 명사 받을 때
(단수명사와 결합가능)–<u>단수취급</u>

셀 수 있는 명사 만을 받는 대명사
셀 수 있는 복수명사와 결합가능–복수취급

셀 수 없는 명사 만을 받는 대명사
셀 수 없는 단수명사와 결합가능–<u>단수취급</u>

모두 <u>all</u> (N)

대부분 <u>most</u> (N)

<u>many</u> (N)
<u>a good many</u> (N)
a number/numbers [of 복수명사]

많은 것
a lot/lots [of 단/복수명사]
<u>plenty</u> (N)

<u>much</u> (N)
a good deal [of 단수명사]
a large amount [of 단수명사]

절반
<u>(a/the) half</u> (N)

얼마간
<u>some/any</u> (N)

<u>several</u> (N)

여럿

<u>a few</u> (N)

약간

<u>a little</u> (N)

<u>few</u> (N)

거의 없는

<u>little</u> (N)

하나도 없는
none [of 단/복수명사]
no 명사

Study 01 many, a few, few & much, a little, little

셀 수 있는 명사에 사용하는 것	셀 수 있는 명사와 셀 수 없는 명사 모두 사용	셀 수 없는 명사에 사용하는 것
many 많은 수	a lot/lots (of) 많은 수/많은 양	much 많은 양
a few 2~3개의	_____	a little 약간의
few	거의 없는	little

⊙ many, a few, few는 셀 수 있는 명사와 사용할 수 있다. 반면에 much, a little, little 셀 수 없는 명사 만 사용할 수 있다. a lot, lots, plenty는 셀 수 있는 명사, 셀 수 없는 명사 모두와 사용할 수 있다.

1. 셀 수 있는 명사와 사용될 수 있는 것들: many, a few, few

① few; 거의 없는

• **Few** girls have a ponytail like that.　　　저 사람처럼 묶어 늘어뜨린 머리를 가진 소녀가 거의 없다.

• There are **few** things simpler yet more functional than the paper bag.

　　　　　　　종이백보다 더 단순하지만 더 기능적인 것들이 거의 없다.

② a few: 2~3개 있는

- Here are **a few** tips for you.　　　　　너를 위한 몇 가지 정보가 여기에 있다.

- Sylvette was sitting with **a few** friends on the terrace in the sun.

　　　　　　　　Sylvette는 태양이 내리쬐는 테라스에서 몇몇 친구들과 앉아 있는 중이다.

- It might be a good idea to stay away from the computer for **a few** days.

　　　　　　　　몇일 동안 컴퓨터와 멀리 떨어져 있는 것은 좋은 생각이다.

- May I ask **a few** questions about the cell phone you bought last week?

　　　　　　　　내가 지난번에 네가 산 휴대폰에 관해 몇 가지 질문해도 될까요?

③ many: 많은

- You have **many** marvelous pets.　　　　　너는 몇 마리의 멋진 애완동물을 가지고 있구나.

- Still, for **many** Koreans, wearing a Hanbok is a way of showing pride in their history and culture.

　　　　그러나 많은 한국인들에게 한복을 입는 것은 그들의 역사와 문화에 있어서 자존심을 보여주는 방식이다.

2. 셀 수 없는 명사와 쓰일 수 있는 것: much, a little, little

① little: 거의 없는

- He showed **little** interest in Tesla's idea.　　　　그는 테슬라의 생각에 거의 관심을 보이지 않았다.

② a little: 약간 있는

- There is **a little** stationery in this classroom.　　　이 교실에는 약간의 문구류가 있다

① much: 많은

- You know for that <u>much</u> money you can get a much better one.

그 같은 많은 돈으로 훨씬 좋은 것을 얻을 수 있다.

CF	비교급에서 '훨씬'이라는 뜻으로 쓰인다.
	이때 much는 far, by far, still, even, a lot으로 대신 쓸 수 있다.

- The bears, especially females, are now <u>much</u> thinner. 그 곰들 특히 암컷들은 지금 훨씬 야위었다.
- Visiting Namsangol Hanok Village in Seoul would be a <u>much</u> better idea.

서울에서 남산골 한복마을을 방문하는 것은 훨씬 좋은 생각일 것이다.

 확인문제 1

다음 문장의 빈칸에 few, a few, little, a little 중 알맞은 것을 쓰시오.

(01). I'll give you another phone call in (   ) days.

(02). I'd like to have (   ) friends who can understand me.

(03). There is nothing to see in that village, so (   ) tourists visit here.

(04). The old man couldn't read and write because he had (   ) education.

(05). They are having (   ) difficulty, but the problem is not so serious.

〈정답과 해설 30P〉

 확인문제 2

다음 a lot of 나 lots of를 대신 사용할 수 있는 것을 much나 many 중 하나를 쓰시오.

(01). The dresses have <u>lots of</u> modern features like buttons.

(02). He gave me <u>a lot of</u> advice about the role that I played.

(03). <u>Lots of</u> famous people in history had strange sleeping habits.

(04). As you know, <u>a lot of</u> children are dying from hunger all over the world.

(05). We can see and experience <u>lots of</u> things about Korean culture in the Folk Village.

〈정답과 해설 30P〉

Level UP

셀 수 있는 명사와 셀 수 없는 명사

명사는 셀 수 있는 명사와 셀 수 없는 명사로 나뉜다. 보통 셀 수 있는 명사는 하나일 때, a(n)을 쓰고 둘 이상일 때 명사에 -(e)s를 쓴다. 셀 수 없는 명사는 a(n)도 붙이지 않고 복수형도 만들지 않는다.

many, a few, few와 함께 사용될 수 있는 것 (셀 수 있는 명사)	much, a little, little과 함께 사용될 수 있는 것 (셀 수 없는 명사)
• 보통명사 - 보통 단수는 a(n)을 사용하고 　　　　　복수는 -(e)s를 쓴다. a speaker-speakers, a bag-bags a clock-clocks, a watch-watches • 셀 수 있는 추상명사- 형태가 없는 추상명사이지만 구체적 행위나 상황을 나타내는 말로 셀 수 있다. 보통 명사처럼 보통 단수는 a(n)을 사용하고 복수는 -(e)s를 쓸 수 있다. a war-wars, a way-ways, a skill-skills a job-jobs, a hobby-hobbies, • 집합덩어리와 구성원들 두 가지로 사용되는 것: 하나의 집합덩어리는 단수, 구성원을 가리킬 때는 복수취급 한다. 또 집합덩어리가 여러 개 일 때는 복수로 쓴다. 　family(가족-단수, 가족구성원들-복수)-families (여러)가족들, class(학급-단수, 학생들-복수)-classes(여러)학급들	• 물질명사(고체, 액체, 기체) 고체- waste, iron, wood, gold, stone 액체- water, coffee 기체- air, gas 주의) 여러 잡탕의 고체물질로 이루어진 셀 수 없는 명사 clothing의류, furniture가구, stationery문구류 baggage수화물, equipment장비 machinery기계류, merchandise상품 • 개념을 말하는 셀 수 없는 추상명사 advice, information, hope, peace, belief money, freedom, life, love, truth, kindness beauty, friendship 주의) -s가 붙어있으나 원래 단어가 그렇게 생겼을 뿐 복수가 아닌 것 news, means수단, measles홍역 economics경제학, physics물리학

A. –(e)s없는 복수형 명사

children아이들, men남자들, women여성들, sheep양들, deer사슴들, fish 물고기들
people(사람들) the police(경찰관들), my family(나의 가족들)처럼 구성원을 가리키는 복수명사들도 있다.

• My family are very happy.   나의 가족들은 매우 행복하다.

B. 복수형태이고 복수취급하는 좌우대칭형명사

대칭을 이루는 단어로 복수 형태인 glasses안경, pants팬츠, trousers바지 등 복수로 쓰고 복수취급 한다.

• My sunglasses are good for eye protection.   나의 선글라스는 눈보호를 위하여 좋다.

C. 온갖 잡탕으로 이루어진 셀 수 없는 명사

영어에서 '셀 수 있는 명사란 비슷비슷한 모양을 가진 여러 개가 있는 경우'를 말한다. 하지만 furniture(a chair, a desk, a bookcase 등으로 구성) 가구류, clothing(a suit, pants, trousers, a shirt 등으로 구성) 의류, stationery(a notebook, a pen, a pencil 등) 문구류, machinery(a bus, a computer, a telephone, a clock 등으로 구성) 기계류, equipment(스키장비, 골프장비, 등산장비 등 여러 장비들로 구성) 장비류, merchandise(a watch, an air conditioner, a book, a smart phone 등 여러 상품으로 구성) 상품, baggage/luggage수하물 등은 여러 가지 모양을 가진, 온갖 잡탕으로 이루어진 것들로 셀 수 없는 명사이다.

• Much clothing piles up in the store.	많은 의류가 가게에 쌓여 있다.
• There is some furniture in the room.	그방안에 몇몇 가구류가 있다.

Study 02 all, most, a lot/lots, half, some, none 등

⊙ 셀 수 있는 명사와 셀 수 없는 명사 모두와 쓸 수 있는 표현들이다. 셀 수 없는 명사와 쓰이면 단수취급하고 셀 수 있는 명사와 쓰이면 복수한다.

1. 셀 수 없는 명사와 결합- 단수

- **All** the food is supplied by the residents.
- **A lot** of machinery is ready for the project.
- **Some** of the clothing was made in Italy.
- **Half** of the equipment is demanded for helping the accident.

모든 음식은 주민들에 의해 제공된다.
많은 기계류가 그 프로젝트에 준비된다.
얼마간의 의류가 이태리에서 만들어진다.

그 장비의 반이 그 사고를 돕는데 요구된다.

2. 셀 수 있는 명사의 복수형태와 결합-복수

- **A lot** of fans follow the actors
- **Half** of the books are supplied for the citizens.
- **Some** of the cars were made in Korea.
- **All** the friends are supporters for democracy.

많은 팬들이 그 배우를 따른다
책들의 반이 시민들을 위해 공급된다
그 차들의 반이 한국에서 만들어 진다

모든 학생들이 민주주의를 위한 지지자들이다.

확인문제 3

다음 문장에서 각각 알맞은 말을 쓰시오.

(01). (Is / Are) all the food for the party ready?

(02). All the guests (is / are) waiting for you.

(03). Most the students (have / has) their own merit.

(04). Why (is / are) most the students in the late today?

(05). Most the stationery (is/ are) on stock in the storage.

(06). Some of the audience (was/ were) moved by the play.

(07). Some of the candidates (has/ have) already presented their speeches.

(08). Some of the clothing in our store (was/ were) flooded last week.

(09). Most the employees (was/ were) in a business meeting.

(10). All the athletes (trains/ train) for the upcoming World cup in this stadium.

world cup

〈정답과 해설 30P〉

Study 03 some(thing, body)과 any(thing, body)

some(thing, body)	any(thing, body)
긍정문, 다만 의문문 형식이지만 권유나 확인을 위한 긍정적 답 유도할 때 some(thing, body)가 쓰인다.	의문문, 부정문, 조건문 다만, 긍정문에서도 '어떤~라도'의 뜻으로 쓰일 경우 any(thing, body)가 쓰인다.

1. some

① 긍정문
- Yes, I'll bring you **some** food.
- Here are **some** tips for you.
- I'd like to rent **some** toys for my little son.

예, 너에게 얼마간의 음식을 가지고 올게요.
너를 위한 얼마간의 정보가 여기 있어요.

나는 나의 어린 아들을 위하여 얼마간의 장난감을 빌리고 싶어요.

② 권유나 긍정적 답 유도(확인)
- Would you like **some** water?
- Do you have **some** food?

물 좀 드세요.(권유)
음식 좀 가지고 있지요? (확인).

2. any

① 의문문
- Are there **any** magazines to read?

읽을 잡지들 있어요?

② 부정문
- I don't have **any** plans this weekend yet.

나는 이번 주 아직 어떠한 계획도 없어요.

3. 조건문

• If you have **any** problems, call me at once.

네가 어떤 문제가 있다면 즉시 나에게 전화하세요.

CF 긍정문에서 '어떠한 ~라도'의 뜻으로 쓰인다.

• You can take **any** bus here.

너는 여기에서 어떠한 버스라도 탈 수 있어요.

• The beggar can eat **anything** on the dish.

그 거지는 그 접시에 어떤 것이라도 먹을 수 있다.

 **확인문제 4**

다음 문장의 빈칸에 some이나 any 중 알맞은 것을 쓰시오.

(01). Do you have _____ good ideas?

(02). They don't have _____ classes on Saturday.

(03). The poor kid needs _____ paper and pencils.

(04). The old lady doesn't have _____ brothers or sisters.

(05). Do your friends have _____ special plans for tonight?

(06). Would you like _____ coffee or green tea?

(07). The workers should take _____ rest.

(08). Are there _____ animals in this park?

(09). The beggar put _____ coins in the bending machine.

(10). Would you like to have _____ ice cream or bread?

〈정답과 해설 30P〉

Grammar in Reading

〈정답과 해설 30~31P〉

1. 다음 밑줄 친 ⓐ~ⓔ 중 어색한 부분을 모두 찾아 고치시오.

A: Did our group miss ⓐ much questions?

B: No, you didn't. but your group missed ⓑ a little questions.

A: Can I ask you ⓒ a little questions?

B: I'm sorry, but I don't have ⓓ much time now.

　Why don't you come to me tomorrow with your group members?

A: Sure. I will see you with ⓔ a little friends.

2. 아래 (　　　) 안에 알맞은 말과 같은 단어가 들어가는 것은 몇 번인가?

Here's the weather forecast for Chicago.

There was (　　　) electricity available where they lived, and they also couldn't afford batteries for radios. They were cut off from the rest of society, unable to hear any news about what was going on in the outside world.

01. She has (　　　) friends.

02. (　　　) boys used to jump to the river.

03. Herry has (　　　) books in her bag.

04. Here are (　　　) tips to sleep well.

05. There is (　　　) clothing in the cottage.

3. 아래 글의 빈칸에 little, a little, few, a few 중에서 알맞은 말을 넣으시오.

In the past, very (　　　) women were successful in American politics. Those who achieved high position did so because their family had the position before them. Ella Grasso, however, was different.

Grammar in Reading

〈정답과 해설 31P〉

4. 다음 (   ) 안에 알맞은 것을 고르시오.

Hello, everyone. This is Eric Adams from the evening news. Today I'd like to introduce a very meaningful concert. The title is 'Heal the Future.' This event is sponsored by Hope for Children, one of the largest children's rights organizations in our country. 'Heal the Future' includes performances by ⓐ(many, much) famous singers and movie stars. The concert director says that all the performers ⓑ(is/are) ready to bring people a wonderful evening. 'Heal the Future' will be held on June 28 and performed at HFC's Hall. All the profits of this concert will go to a local orphanage. To purchase tickets, visit the homepage, www. hopeforchildren.com.

01. ⓐ–

02. ⓑ–

5. 다음 (   ) 안에 알맞은 것을 고르시오.

Kevin's mother has always wanted to study Spanish, so she starts taking a lesson. Kevin is happy that his mother is trying to learn ⓐ(something, anything) new. One day, Kevin asks her if she's doing well with her studying. She says that she's trying hard but she has a problem. She can't find enough time to study because of housework. Kevin wants to support his mother, so he decides to do ⓑ(some, any) housework for her.

01. ⓐ –

02. ⓑ –

Grammar in Reading

〈정답과 해설 31P〉

6. 다음 (   ) 안에 알맞는 말을 고르시오.

"Buy Nothing Day" is on the fourth Friday of November. On this day, ⓐ(many, much) people in about 40 countries don't buy ⓑ(something, anything). "Buy nothing" means "make no trash." When you make less trash, you can make a cleaner earth.

"Meat out Day" is on March 20. Many people from around the world don't eat ⓒ(some, any) meat for one day. Join this day, and you will get healthier. Also, you can reduce greenhouse gases and save the earth.

Many people are trying to save the earth with special days like "Earth Day," "Buy Nothing Day" and "Meatout Day." Do you want to join them? Then you should remember these special days and do ⓓ(something, anything) green.

01. ⓐ -
02. ⓑ -
03. ⓒ -
04. ⓓ -

〈정답과 해설 32P〉

1. 다음 빈칸에 올 수 없는 단어를 모두 고르시오.

01. The king has much ( ) in his house.
① money ② books ③ clothing ④ shoes ⑤ machinery

02. The president's wife has many ( ) in her house.
① skirts ② furniture ③ shoes ④ glasses ⑤ clothing

03. There are a few ( ) in the restaurant.
① customers ② wine ③ dishes ④ glasses ⑤ plates

04. There are a few ( ) in the hotel room.
① people ② phones ③ clothing ④ computers ⑤ stationery

05. The man has little ( ) in his house.
① food ② money ③ water ④ books ⑤ paper

2. 다음 문장의 잘못된 부분이 있는 문장을 찾아 올바로 고쳐 쓰시오.

01. She didn't have many food.
→ _____

02. I have a little good friends.
→ _____

03. There is a few juice in the glass.
→ _____

04. He gave the poor boy a little money.
→ _____

05. There are a little books on the table.
→ _____

〈정답과 해설 32P〉

06. The doctor doesn't have many hope for the man's illness.

 → _____

07. The thief has been reading this book for a little days.

 → _____

08. Alex and his brother used to exercise for much hours a day.

 → _____

09. There are much ducks on the lake.

 → _____

10. The old woman has many friends in my town.

 → _____

11. There are not much people in the park.

 → _____

12. I have a little time and money right now.

 → _____

13. We can see much snow in winter.

 → _____

14. There are a little glasses on the table.

 → _____

15. I have a few history books.

 → _____

16. The woman threw a few fish to the rock for the baby seal.

 → _____

〈정답과 해설 32P〉

3. 다음 중 어법상 어색한 부분을 찾아 바르게 고쳐 쓰시오.

01. There is many people in the theater.
  → _____

02. There is a lot of milks in the bottle.
  → _____

03. She has a little pretty dolls.
  → _____

04. Much animals are in the zoo.
  → _____

05. He ate too many bread.
  → _____

06. There is a lot of water in the glass.
  → _____

07. Inho and Susan drink a lot of milk.
  → _____

08. Much students watch too much TV.
  → _____

09. Teenagers do many things because of peer pressure.
  → _____

10. The princess has many clothing in her house.
  → _____

〈정답과 해설 32P〉

4. 다음 문장에서 (   ) 안에 little, a little, few, a few, many와 much 중 하나를 쓰시오.

01. We have (   ) new toys here.

02. There are (   ) buildings for offices and living.

03. Does she have (   ) collected information?

04. Making a presentation requires (   ) preparation.

05. I think there are (   ) good points about Hanbok.

06. Due to the sudden heavy snow, (   ) people arrived at the meeting on time.

07. Can I have (   ) talk with you now? I've got something important to tell you.

08. There were (   ) suggestions that I couldn't accept. I'd like to talk about them now.

09. No one knew that yesterday was Brendon's birthday. He had (   ) friends in his school.

10. His sister had a stomachache this morning, so she could have (   ) food.

5. many와 much 중 하나를 쓰시오.

01. (   ) teens don't get enough sleep.

02. Women have (   ) beer these days.

03. Are there (   ) kids in the park?

04. There isn't (   ) time to waste.

05. How (   ) water do you drink a day?

〈정답과 해설 32P〉

06. I really like to see as (   ) places as I can in Seoul.

07. There were as (   ) blue whales in the 19th century as there are now.

08. (   ) worried people are gathering now to watch the burning gate.

09. There are (   ) watering pots here, honey.

10. Most important thing is to get as (   ) reliable information as you can before spending your money.

6. 다음 중 어법상 맞지 않는 것을 찾아 올바르게 고치시오.

01. Just a little pages were left.

02. How much are the books? 〈가격을 묻는 표현〉

03. Your cart has too many items.

04. We saw lots of stars at night.

05. I missed Sally so much.

06. I'll give him a shot and many medicine.

07. I bought this book a few days ago.

08. We have learned much expressions.

09. Edison showed few interest in it.

10. A professor had little friends.

11. Tesla made few money from his inventions.

12. David spent a lot of money. He has few money now.

13. I'd like to tell you a few bit about the museum.

14. There are several cushion on a very comfortable armchair.

15. This is a kind of sales technique many salespeople use.

7. 다음 중 어법상 맞지 않는 것을 찾아 올바르게 고치시오.

01. Would you like to have any pizza?

02. There are any eggs in the refrigerator.

03. Were there some phone calls for me?

04. Do you know any famous movie stars?

05. We have someone to eat lunch with.

06. I'm really sorry, but I have some work to do.

07. Some students refuse to obey the school's policy.

08. I'm very hungry, but I don't have some food to eat.

09. Did you eat all my candies? There aren't some candies left!

10. You shouldn't take any medicine without reading the information first.

중간·기말고사 내신만점대비문제

〈정답과 해설 32~33P〉

8. 다음 문장에서 some과 any중 하나를 쓰시오.

01. Can I have (   ) tea please?

02. Would you like (   ) hot coffee?

03. There aren't (   ) parks in my city.

04. There are (   ) nice pictures in this book

05. There aren't (   ) oranges on the market.

06. We don't have (   ) tests in this term.

07. The fisher caught (   ) fishes in this river.

08. Do you have (   ) brothers or sisters?

09. Do you have (   ) tests in the summer term?

10. Is there (   ) furniture in your office?

11. There isn't (   ) milk in the refrigerator.

12. I'm here to buy (   ) fruit for Mr. Jackson.

13. Mr. Jackson bought (   ) flowers for him.

14. Please buy (   ) ice cream at the supermarket.

15. Do you have (   ) homework in this weekend?

16. I can't make a cake because we don't have (   ) eggs.

17. The old writer got (   ) postcards from readers.

〈정답과 해설 33P〉

18. My daughters didn't spend _____ money today.

19. Jane bought _____ books, but she didn't buy _____ pens.

20. _____ bus will take you King's Cross, so get on the first that comes along.

9. 다음 문장에서 (   ) 안에 알맞은 것을 고르시오.

01. After (few/ a few/ little/ a little) weeks, you should be able to determine which time is best for you.

02. In my opinion, it's (very/ much/ many) easier to learn how to do things when you're young.

03. (Some/ Any) of my friends teased me by pushing me into a pool, and I almost drowned.

04. Dandy is a young male chimpanzee. Recently, he did (something/ anything) that surprised many scientists.

05. (Some/ Any) parents write resumes, attend job fairs, and chat with career counselors for their children.

06. Stress hormones increase when you work out, then drop back down after (a little/ a few) hours.

07. Experts say those who have at least one daily meal with a family enjoy (much/ many) benefits.

08. The lesson here is that with (a little/ a few) creativity, a mistake can be a chance for success.

09. According to (some/ any) experts, helicopter parenting can prevent young people from developing their self-confidence and independence.

Chapter

10

Pronouns & Nouns 2
구체적으로 지정하는 대명사
It(they), one(ones)
the one, the other 등

Study 01 it(복수일 때 they)와 one(복수일 때 ones)

it과 they는 구체적으로 지정된 것을 말한다. 하나일 때 it, 둘 이상일 때 they로 쓴다.

그에 비하여 one과 ones는 어떤 명사 구체적으로 지정하지 않고 그 종류만을 말한다. 단수 일때, one, 복수일 때 ones를 쓴다.

특정한 것(들)	특정하지 않은 것(들)
it –they(them)	one–ones cf> one은 일반인 '사람들'으로 사용 할 수 있다.

1. it와 they

◉ 예를 들면, 그 책(들) 등 구체적으로 지칭할 때 쓴다.

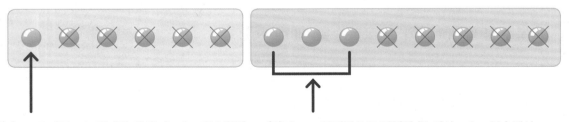

(1) it: 구체적으로 정해진 것 하나– the 단수명사

(2) they: 구체적으로 정해진 둘 이상 – the 복수명사

- A: Would you like to buy the car?

  B: Yes, I would buy it.

  그 차를 사시겠어요?

  예, 나는 그 차를 살게요.

- A: I bought some novels in the internet bookstore yesterday. **They** are very exciting.

  어제 인터넷 서점에서 몇 권의 소설을 샀다. 그들은 매우 재미있다.

  B: Please lend me **them**.

2. one과 ones

⊙ 예를들면, 명사를 구체적인 지칭없이 그냥 책(들) 등을 말할 때 쓴다.

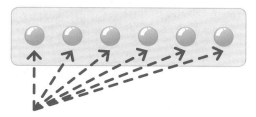

(1) one: 구체적으로 정해지지 않은 하나 – a(n) 단수명사

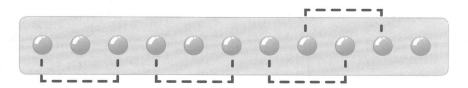

(2) ones: 구체적으로 정해지지 않은 둘이상 – 복수명사

• A: Would you like to have a hamburger?　　햄버거를 하나 드시겠어요?
  B: Yes, I would like **one**. (or) Yes, I would like to have **ones**.

　　　　　　　　　　　　예, 햄버거 하나 먹고 싶어요, (혹은) 예, 나는 햄버거들 먹고 싶다.

 일반인을 나타내는 one

• **One** should be honest.　　　　　　사람은 정직해야 한다.

[보기]에서 알맞은 단어를 골라 빈칸에 쓰시오.

| [보기] | one | ones | it | them |

(01). A: Did you see my smart phone?
　　　B: Oh, I was using (　　　　). Sorry.

(02). A: They have only yellow flowers.
　　　B: We want red (　　　　).

(03). Katie bought a small car, but I wanted a big (　　　　).

(04). (　　　　) usually finds that friendship is very important.

(05). We need a table for meeting. Do you have (　　　　)?

(06). Teddy has a nice bicycle. You have (　　　　), too.

(07). Are these books yours?
　　　– No, mine are the (　　　　) on the desk.

(08). (　　　　) should preserve natural resource for the future.

〈정답과 해설 33P〉

Study 02 one/the one/the other/another/ some/others/the others

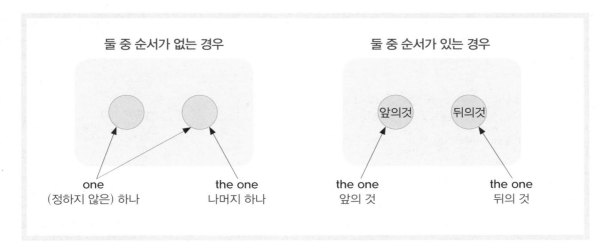

둘 중 순서가 없는 경우

one
(정하지 않은) 하나

the one
나머지 하나

둘 중 순서가 있는 경우

앞의것

뒤의것

the one
앞의 것

the one
뒤의 것

- My younger sister has two pet dogs; **one** is small, but **the other** is large.
  내 여동생은 두마리의 애완견을 가지고 있다. 한마리는 작고 나머지 한마리는 크다.

- I have a sister and a brother; **the one** is smart, and **the other** is strong.
  나는 누이와 형제가 한명씩 있다. 누이는 영리하고, 형제는 강하다.

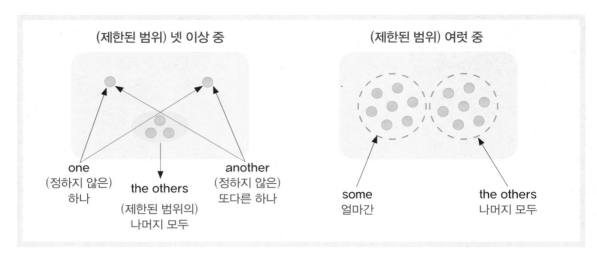

- I don't like this **one**. Show me **another**.

  저는 이것이 마음에 들지 않아요. 다른 것을 보여 주세요.

- May I have **another** cup of tea?

  차 한잔 더 마실 수 있을 까요?

- I have three roses. **One** is red, **another** is pink, and **the other** is white.

  나는 세 개의 장미를 가지고 있습니다. 하나는 빨강색, 또 다른 하나는 핑크색, 나머지 하나는 하얀색입니다.

- 50 members participate in the camping. **some** want to play baseball, while **the others** want to play soccer.

  50명 의 회원들이 캠핑에 참여한다. 얼마간의 사람들은 야구하는 것을 원한다. 반면에 다른 사람들은 축구를 하는 것을 원한다.

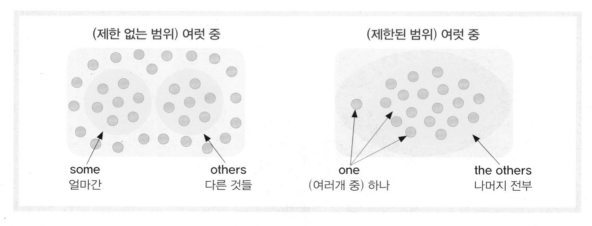

- **Some** supported the Democratic party candidate while **others** supported the Republic party candidate.

  얼마간의 사람들은 민주당 후보를 지지한 반면에 다른 사람들은 공화당후보를 지지했다.

- There are four pets in my house. **One** is a dog, **another** is an iguana and **the others** are parrots.

  집에 네 마리의 애완동물이 있다. 하나는 개이고 또 다른 하나는 이구아나, 나머지 두 마리는 앵무새다.

다음 각 문장에서 빈칸에 알맞은 것을 고르시오.

(01). Please, show me (another, other) bike.

(02), The movie director gave me (other, another) chance.

(03). Do you have any (other, another) magazines?

(04). We should be kind to (another, others).

(05). One of the twins is my friend. I don't know (the other, others).

(06). Here are two rabbits. One is mine and (the other, another) is his.

(07). I saw only Alex and Becky. Where are (the other, the others)?

(08). I bought ten balls. Two of them are red. (The others, Others) are yellow.

(09). Don't care too much about what (others, the other) say about it.

(10). Anasazi entered the room, and (other, another) girls followed him.

〈정답과 해설 33P〉

Grammar in Reading

〈정답과 해설 33~34P〉

1. 다음 (   ) 안에 알맞은 것을 고르시오.

M: Welcome. How may I help you?
W: My car has been recently making strange sounds since I had an accident.
M: Okay. Any other problems?
W: Well, sometimes the air conditioner and the CD player don't work well.
M: All right. I'll check ⓐ(them, ones) out.
W: Thanks. Do you know if my insurance will cover the repairs?
M: I'm not sure. Why don't you call the insurance company?
W: I will. How long will the repairs take?
M: There are ⓑ(a few, a little) things to look at, so it may take about an hour.
W: Do I have to stay here? I need to take my dog to the vet.
M: No, you don't have to. I'll call you to let you know what repairs are needed.
W: That would be great. Thanks.

01. ⓐ –   02. ⓑ –

2. 다음 (   ) 안에 알맞은 것을 고르시오.

W: I'm planning to hike Ji-ri mountain this weekend.
M: Really? I didn't know you liked hiking.
W: I don't go hiking very often. So I need your advice.
M: Okay. Remember safety comes first. You need to start hiking early since darkness arrives
　 ⓐ(much, many) quicker in the mountains.
W: That makes sense.
M: You should carry a small flashlight for that reason.
W: I see. Do you think I need to take a map or a guidebook?
M: Absolutely. You need a map to keep track of where you are on the mountain.
W: I'll buy ⓑ(it, one) on my way home, then. What else should I know?
M: Don't forget to take a first aid kit, just in case.
W: Okay, I will. Thanks for all your ⓒ(tip, tips).
M: You're welcome. I hope you'll enjoy the hike.

01. ⓐ –   02. ⓑ –   03. ⓒ –

Grammar in Reading

〈정답과 해설 34P〉

3. 다음 (   ) 안에 알맞은 것을 고르시오.

Recently, there have been ⓐ(much, many) complaints about dogs barking late at night. This has been a major concern, especially to those who have to go to work early the next morning. Last night ⓑ(it, one) happened again, and eventually the police had to come to our apartments to deal with ⓒ(it, one). Furthermore, ⓓ (much, many)residents have been complaining about people not cleaning up after their dogs. I urge you to take the necessary actions about these complaints. Please make sure your dogs do not bark at night. Also, in order to maintain a clean and pleasant environment, please pick up after your pets. Thanks for listening.

01. ⓐ -   02. ⓑ -   03. ⓒ -
04. ⓓ -

※ [4-9] 아래 글을 읽고 괄호 안에 one, another, some, any, other, others, the other, the others 중 알맞은 것을 넣으시오.

4.

Hi, I'm Lee Jinsu, your listener.
Yesterday, we had a basketball game with ⓐ(   ) class and lost the game.
The other team's players were tall and talented. I want to grow taller, but I don't know how. Is there ⓑ(   ) good way? Please let me know if there is.

01. ⓐ-   02. ⓑ-

5.

The pyramids were built for Egyptian Kings and queens. The Egyptians believed that there was an afterlife. The Egyptians also believed that the pharaohs were living gods. The pyramids were designed to provide these kings with everything they would need to make a journey to (   ) life.

Grammar in Reading

〈정답과 해설 34~35P〉

6.

Although there is clear evidence that the pyramids were built as tombs, all kinds of strange claims have been made about them. ⓐ(   ) people have claimed that the pyramids were used to watch the moon and stars. ⓑ(   ) have even claimed that the pyramids were built by aliens

01. ⓐ-   02. ⓑ-

7.

In ⓐ(   ) cultures, the meaning of an advertisement is delivered by the exact words. This is true in many Western countries such as the United States and Britain. But in ⓑ(   ) cultures, such as in Korea or Japan, the message depends more on situations and feelings than the words.

01. ⓐ-   02. ⓑ-

Grammar in Reading

〈정답과 해설 34~35P〉

8.

There are many different kinds of animals in the world. All animals aren't the same, of course. ⓐ( ) animals have a backbone, while ⓑ( ) don't. ⓒ( ) have hair, ⓓ( ) don't. However, each one helps make our world a wild and wonderful place.

01. ⓐ–   02. ⓑ–   03. ⓒ–
04. ⓓ–

9.

With the invention of portable tape recorders, scientists started to study birdsong. Birds usually make two kinds of sounds: calls and songs. Calls are short and simple sounds, but songs are longer and more musical. Usually only male birds sing, and they sing for two purposes. ⓐ( ) is keeping their territory. and ⓑ( ) is a finding mate.

01.ⓐ–   02.ⓑ–

1. [보기]에서 알맞은 단어를 골라 빈칸에 쓰시오.

> **[보기]**　one　ones　it　they　them

01. There are white rabbits and black (　　　　).

02. Karry has some red roses and white (　　　　).

03. Alice wants a white smart phone and Ted wants (　　　　).

04. The children went camping and (　　　) got lost last year.

05. I will go to the stationery shop to buy an eraser, do you want (　　　　)?

06. Jane has a red dress, but she wants a blue (　　　　).

07. Robert took the papers and threw (　　　) away.

08. Did you see his books? – Yes, I put (　　　　) on the bookcase.

2. 아래 문장에서 각각 알맞은 것을 골라 넣으시오.

> **[보기]**　one　another　some　the other　others　the others

01. Mary has two caps. One is big, and (　　　) is small.

02. Some like dogs, but (　　　) don't like them.

03. Mom invited ten people to her birthday party. Some came, but (　　　) didn't.

04. There are three tables. One is red, another is brown, and (　　　) is black.

05. Look at the two cats. (　　　) is small, and(　　　) is big.

〈정답과 해설 35P〉

06. John has five sons. (   ) like basketball, and (   ) like soccer.

07. Do you see the three boys there? One is tall, (   ) is short, and (   ) is thin.

08. Some believe in God while (   ) don't believe at all.

09. I have two sweaters. (   ) is blue, and (   ) is red.

10. Some people go jogging in the morning, and (   ) go jogging at night.

11. Mr. Hwang has three children. (   ) is Mimi, another is Sumi, and (   ) is Boyoung.

12. There are a lot of people in the airport. (   ) are Chinese, (   ) are Japanese.

13. I got three flowers. (   ) was a rose, (   ) was a lily, and the other was a sunflower.

14. Henry has two sisters. (   ) is 10 years old, and (   ) is 8 years old.

15. There are a dozen books. (   ) are English, and(   ) are Korean.

16. "The dragon will help us soon," said (   ) child. "He must do something," agreed (   ).

저자 손창연 선생님 강의 수강 후기들!!

-홈페이지에 실명으로 올린 내용들이나 이름 가운데를 ♥처리 합니다.-

스탠포드 재학생 김♥원

포드 대학 3학년 재학중인 학생입니다. 수강 후기를 쓰기 전, 저는 선생님과 그전에 아무런 연고도 없었고 본 학원과 금전적으로 아무런 연관이 없다는 것을 분명히 밝힙니다.

제가 손창연 선생님께 문법을 배운것이 중학교 때였는데, 그때까지만 해도 Writing이 많이 부족하고 영어 내신 시험에서도 까다로운 문법 문제를 꼭 한두개씩 틀려오곤 했습니다. 그러다 어느 날 영문학을 전공하신 아버지께서 서점에서 책을 사 가지고 오시며, 당신이 본 문법책 중에 제일 논리적으로 정리가 잘 되어있으니 꼭 한 번 보라고 말씀하셨습니다. 그 책이 바로 〈뼈에 사무치는 영어문법〉이었습니다.

그렇게 하여 손창연쌤 논리영어에 등록을 하게 되었는데, 다녀본 문법 학원들 중에서 가장 만족했습니다. 무조건 외우는 문법이 아니라 논리와 암기가 잘 조화된 학습 방법 덕에 문법 체계가 확실히 잡히게 되었습니다. 중요한 내용을 반복적으로 강조하시고 큰 그림을 잘 그려주셔서 그 때 배운 문법과 예문들이 아직도 머릿속에 떠오릅니다.

그렇게 하고 나니 대원외고에 진학해서도 영어 학원을 따로 다니지 않아도 내신이 항상 잘 나왔고, 스탠포드에 와서도 에세이를 쓸 때 문법적 오류는 거의 내지 않습니다. 선생님이 하라는 대로 잘 따라하고 책에 있는 예문들을 열심히 외워서 영어 문법을 한 번 제대로 다져 놓으면 그 이후로는 정말 편한 것 같습니다. 손창연 쌤은 마음도 정말 따뜻하셔서 학생 개개인을 잘 챙겨주시고 신경써 주십니다.

학생들에게 정말 추천하는 학원이에요!

seeenglish.com